How to Pass

HIGHER

Computing Science

Greg Reid

HODDER
GIBSON
AN HACHETTE UK COMPANY

The Publishers would like to thank the following for permission to reproduce copyright material:

Photo credits p.14 © Monkey Business Images/Stockbroker/Thinkstock; p.24 © fuchs-photography/Thinkstock; p.27 © AF archive/Alamy; p.31 © Shigeru23; p.32 © Andrei Besleaga/Amstrad PLC; p.33 © Jesse Wild/MacFormat Magazine via Getty Images; p.35 PyScripter screengrab published under an MIT licence, https://en.wikipedia.org/wiki/MIT_License; p.58 © Sandia National Laboratories/Photodisc/Getty Images; p.65 top left © CBsigns/Alamy; top right and bottom left © TP/Alamy; bottom right © PSL Images/Alamy

Acknowledgements

The Course Assessment Specification grids in Appendix D (pp. 90–93) are reproduced by permission © Scottish Qualifications Authority.

Every effort has been made to trace all copyright holders, but if any have been inadvertently overlooked the Publishers will be pleased to make the necessary arrangements at the first opportunity.

Although every effort has been made to ensure that website addresses are correct at time of going to press, Hodder Gibson cannot be held responsible for the content of any website mentioned in this book. It is sometimes possible to find a relocated web page by typing in the address of the home page for a website in the URL window of your browser.

Hachette UK's policy is to use papers that are natural, renewable and recyclable products and made from wood grown in sustainable forests. The logging and manufacturing processes are expected to conform to the environmental regulations of the country of origin.

Orders: please contact Bookpoint Ltd, 130 Park Drive, Milton Park, Abingdon, Oxon OX14 4SE. Tel: (44) 01235 827720. Fax: (44) 01235 400454. Lines are open 9.00–5.00, Monday to Saturday, with a 24-hour message answering service. Visit our website at www.hoddereducation.co.uk. Hodder Gibson can be contacted direct on: Tel: 0141 848 1609; Fax: 0141 889 6315; email: hoddergibson@hodder.co.uk.

First published in 2015 by
Hodder Gibson, an imprint of Hodder Education,
An Hachette UK Company
2a Christie Street
Paisley PA1 1NB

Impression number   5 4 3 2

Year   2019 2018 2017 2016

Cover photo © Kirsty Pargeter - Fotolia
Illustrations by Aptara, Inc.
Typeset in 13/15 pt CronosPro-Lt by Aptara, Inc.
Printed in Spain
A catalogue record for this title is available from the British Library.
ISBN 978 1 4718 3603 9

Contents

Coursework and Exam

Appendices

Answers to Questions   94

Exam preparation

By the time they sit a Higher, many students already know what study methods work for them and what it takes to be successful. You may have passed National 5 Computing Science, but it is important to understand that the step up to Higher is demanding and that you may require a different approach (or approaches) to ensure your success. Read on carefully: you might just find the perfect study tip that makes the difference between one grade and the next!

Exam details

- Length: 2 hours
- Marks: 90
  - Section 1: shorter questions (20 marks).
  - Section 2: longer questions, based around a scenario (a total of 70 marks, around 10 marks per question). Each question will have multiple parts (a, b, c, etc.).
- Balance: 45 marks of Software design and development (SDD) questions and 45 marks of Information systems design and development (ISDD) questions.

The basics of revising

How many of the ideas below have you incorporated in your studying?
- Consider the grade you want to achieve. It's important to have a target.
- Devise a study plan and stick to it. Don't let yourself get distracted. Half an hour of focused, uninterrupted work is much more effective than two hours spent revising while texting and checking Facebook.
- Consider what you can do without. Effective study is time consuming. Is finding out who has died in your favourite soap as important as getting the grades for the college or university place you want?
- Look after yourself. Sleep well, eat well and avoid other stressful situations. Studying and exams can be stressful enough.
- Find out as much as you can about the exam and practise for it. This book will help you with this.
- Know your course. The SQA publishes course outlines for teachers; these can be accessed by anyone. You can use the outline as a checklist of what you have to learn. The list is reproduced in Appendix D (page 88) of this book, or can be found on pages 10–13 of the Course Assessment Specification document at http://www.sqa.org.uk/sqa/56924.html.

Why use practice exam questions?

The famous Chinese philosopher Confucius said, 'The essence of knowledge is, having it, to apply it; not having it, to confess your ignorance.'

Too many students spend an inordinate amount of time while preparing for an exam applying the knowledge they already have. They sit and read notes they understand, answer questions that they already know the answers to – and fail to acknowledge their ignorance of large parts of their course. Take this approach and you will do very well in a small part of your exam only.

The focus of any revision should be to discover what you *don't* know and to use that as your starting point. Take note of the practice exam questions that you can't answer quickly; these will show you what you don't know and therefore what you should research as part of your study.

Understanding the course

Don't leave it too late! To understand a course at Higher level often requires you to understand one fact fully before you move on to the next. If you leave a lesson confused, do something about it. Read over your notes again in the evening, ask your teacher for further explanation, attend study groups, use the internet for research, or even ask your friends for help. Whichever route you take, make sure that you get into this habit early on in the year.

Memorise, memorise, memorise!

Exams require that you retain knowledge throughout the year, meaning that an ability to memorise facts is vital. Don't simply read your notes when you study: research has shown that very few people can read text and remember all of it.

It is difficult to advise students on memory techniques. Everyone has different ways of remembering facts so you'll have to find something that works for you. There are different types of learners, who find that certain common memory techniques work them. These include:

- Reading/writing preference learners: take your own notes, summarising the work you have learned in class. Personalising the work often makes it easier to remember.
- Visual learners: draw diagrams or create concept maps to link facts together in your head.

- Auditory learners: dictate notes into a recording device and regularly listen to the recordings. Many smartphones have apps to record voice notes.
- Kinaesthetic learners: practise practical work. For example, writing programs rather than reading code may greatly improve your ability to understand a coding question in an exam.

There are many websites with hundreds of techniques to try. You'll know you've found techniques that work for you when the standard of your work improves.

Problem solving

A Computing Science exam comprises two question types:

1 Knowledge and Understanding (KU) – these are questions that ask you simply to write down or explain a fact or skill you have learned.
2 Problem Solving (PS) – these are questions where you are required to apply your knowledge to an unfamiliar scenario.

KU questions can easily be prepared for by simply memorising lots of facts. PS questions require practice. Unseen exam questions will go some way towards preparing you for PS questions but you may find that you quickly run out of new examples. Try making up your own question scenarios and swapping them with a friend. Write your own programs or create a database of your own, query it and create a variety of reports from the data. You'll find that the task of making up the questions or scenarios is a problem-solving exercise in itself.

Questions

Note that the questions in this book have been written in a style that may not always resemble those in the Higher exam. The questions have been created to encourage good study, problem solving and research practice. It is recommended that students apply their revision to past paper or sample paper questions as part of their overall revision plan.

And finally…

Commit!

The most pleasing results for teachers are not necessarily the students who get the A grade passes. It's often the students who simply achieve their potential through hard work, even if that is just scraping a pass. Every year teachers see a few students who 'could have done better'. Don't let that be you!

Good luck!

Unit 1 Software Design and Development

Chapter 1

Languages and environments

A computer system is a complex box of electronic components that processes instructions in order to complete given tasks. The writing of these instructions, known as 'programming', requires the use of a programming language. There are many, many different programming languages, each of which was created for a specific purpose (for example business analysis, 3D modelling, database handing, engineering/science work, game programming, artificial intelligence). Some languages have even been created simply to teach programming.

Low level and high level programming languages

All computer processors are manufactured with a set of built-in instructions known as its **instruction set**. Before a program can be executed on a specific processor it must be translated into binary instructions that correspond to the processor's instruction set.

A programmer writing instructions in a **low level language** (LLL) writes program code that corresponds directly to a processor's instruction set.

It is possible for a programmer to write LLL instructions in binary, but this is unlikely due to the difficulty of reading the code and therefore of finding any mistakes that may be made when inputting long lists of 1s and 0s. Most LLL programming is instead carried out using an assembly language that consists of codes that represent each instruction from the instruction set. The codes must still be translated into their binary equivalent before the program can be run.

A **high level language** (HLL) program is written in English, using a strict syntax that defines how each instruction must be formatted. Completed HLL instructions are translated into a separate binary program using a compiler. One set of HLL instructions may be translated into binary programs for different processor instruction sets by using different compilers.

```
mov ah,09h
mov mov dx,offset message
th $
int 21h

mov ah,4ch
mov al,00
int 21h
```

Figure 1.1 A low level language assembly program

```
names = ["Black Beauty","Red Run","Bess","Derek","Philis","Mental","Sissy"]
ages = [12,18,8,5,10,13,19]
height = [13,14,12,15,16,18,14]

maxAge = 0
maxHeight = 0

maxAge = int(input("Please enter the maximum age of the horse"))
maxHeight = int(input("Please enter the maximum height of the horse"))

for loop in range(7):
    if ages[loop] <= maxAge and height[loop] <= maxHeight:
        print (names[loop]+",",ages[loop],"years ,"+height[loop],"hands")
```

Figure 1.2 A high level language Python program

While HLLs provide a simpler way to program computer systems, the binary code produced by compilers is often not as efficient as code written in an LLL. Low level programming is therefore often used for applications where speed of processing or efficient use of resources (for example memory) is an absolute requirement.

High level programming languages can be further categorised as procedural, declarative or object-oriented.

Procedural

A procedural language program is written in blocks of code, called procedures, functions or sub-routines. The program carries out instructions one at a time, calling these procedures as required. The majority of high level languages – Visual Basic, TrueBASIC, Python, Java, PHP, C++ – are procedural languages.

The examples below show how a procedure and a function are written using the SQA's reference language. Although structured in a similar way, a function differs from a procedure in that it returns a value once the code has been executed. A procedure is called with a simple statement – displayMenu(). A function is used as part of an assignment or a condition –SET selection TO userChoice() = 1THEN SET customers = customers + 1

```
PROCEDURE displayMenu()
    SEND "1 — register new customer" TO DISPLAY
    SEND "2 — delete customer record" TO DISPLAY
    SEND "3 — modify customer record" TO DISPLAY
    SEND "4 — end program" TO DISPLAY
END PROCEDURE

FUNCTION userChoice()
    displayMenu()
    SEND "Please enter your choice, 1-4" TO DISPLAY
    REPEAT
        GET choice FROM (INTEGER) KEYBOARD
    UNTIL choice>=1 AND choice<=4
    RETURN choice
END FUNCTION

SET selection TO userChoice()
```

Figure 1.3 A procedural language program

Declarative

A declarative language program is not written as a sequence of instructions. Instead, the code defines a set of logical statements. As the program runs it searches the logical statements for conclusions. Prolog is a declarative programming language used for artificial intelligence applications. A Prolog program defines sets of unordered rules and facts known as a **knowledge base**, which the running program queries for the answers to questions.

```
male(james1).
male(charles1).
male(charles2).
male(james2).
male(george1).

female(catherine).
female(elizabeth).
female(sophia).

parent(charles1, james1).
parent(elizabeth, james1).
parent(charles2, charles1).
parent(catherine, charles1).
parent(james2, charles1).
parent(sophia, elizabeth).
parent(george1, sophia).
```

Figure 1.4 A Prolog knowledge base

Object-oriented

In object-oriented programming, **classes** are defined which include **variables** (these store information on the object) and **methods** (special procedures which define how the object behaves).

Each object created during the execution of an object-oriented program is called an **instance** of a class. New objects will have a copy of the data required to define the object and may inherit data defined in other classes. Object-oriented programming is often used in programs which model real-life situations. New objects can be created, destroyed and modified just as they would in reality.

The example below is taken from a simple game. A class called Player has been created for the player's character. The first procedure defines the object's attributes, the second updates the position of the object using its x and y co-ordinates.

```
class Player(pygame.sprite.Sprite):
    def __init__(self):
        pygame.sprite.Sprite.__init__(self)
        self.rect = pygame.Rect(0, 0, 32, 32)
        self.image = sprite_sheet.subsurface(pygame.Rect(32, 0, 32, 32))

    def update(self, *args):
        """ args[0] = mouse_x
            args[1] = mouse_y """
        self.rect.centerx = args[0]
        self.rect.centery = args[1]
```

Figure 1.5 Object-oriented program code

Game programming is particularly well suited to an object-oriented style of programming, as objects in games (characters, surroundings, weapons and so on) are regularly created and destroyed during gameplay. Note that you are not required to write programs using object-oriented techniques in Higher. Although some computing teachers may prefer to start this early with you, it is only a requirement at Advanced Higher level.

What you should know

In your revision of this chapter, ensure that you are able to:
★ explain the purpose and main characteristics of each category of programming language
★ demonstrate an understanding of the need to translate programs into binary
★ demonstrate the relationship between a computer's instruction set and its program code.

Questions

1 Discuss the statement 'High level language programs are described as platform independent, whereas binary programs are platform specific.' (2)
2 A programmer is asked to write an application for a touchscreen mobile phone. State the type of programming language they are most likely to use and explain your choice. (2)
3 Explain why every programming language has a strict set of rules defining how lines of code should be formatted. (1)
4 Assembly language is a low level language. State why most assembly language instructions still need to be translated into binary. (1)

## Chapter 2

Continuing programming from National 5 to Higher

Professional programmers are constantly immersed in the programming languages with which they work. As a result they rarely forget syntax, can solve easy problems with little effort and can debug most errors very quickly.

In contrast, unless they are keen programmers, students will complete their programming tasks in class, sit an exam and then stop programming. If as a result of this you feel that you have lost some of the skills from National 5, it is important that you are comfortable with the following aspects before you start programming at Higher:

- Creating and manipulating data types (integers, real numbers, strings, Boolean).
- Creating and manipulating arrays.
- Making decisions (complex IF statements using AND, OR and NOT).
- Conditional and unconditional loops.
- Using input validation to ensure only valid values are entered by the user.

Questions

Attempt to write each of the programs below in a programming language of your choice. Test each program to ensure it works as expected. Solutions, in the programming language Python, are given in the Answers section at the back of the book (page 92). If your solution is in a different language you can use the Python code to check that the structure of your program is correct.

1   A collector of antique shoes wishes to put her shoes up for sale. Write a program for her to calculate the total value of her shoes. The program should first ask her how many pairs of shoes she owns and then allow her to enter the price for each pair of shoes. A total cost should be displayed once the data is entered.

2   A parent and child are arguing about which of them watches more TV. Write a program that would allow them to enter the number of hours that each of them watches TV each day for a full week. Once the values have all been entered, the program should calculate whether the parent or the child watches more TV and display an appropriate message.

3   A farmer has been taking pH measurements from soil samples collected from a field. The crop she will plant will depend on whether the average measurement from the field is acidic (pH < 7), neutral (pH = 7) or alkaline (pH > 7). Write a program that will allow each pH measurement (a real number between 0 and 14) to be entered. The user should be asked after each measurement if they wish to enter another measurement. When all the measurements are entered, the program should calculate the average (mean) value and the result (acid, neutral or alkali) should be displayed.

Data types

When programming or demonstrating an understanding of code you will be required to be familiar with the use of single variables to store the following data types:

- Strings – lists of one or more text characters.
- Integers – positive or negative whole numbers.
- Real numbers – positive and negative numbers with decimal places.
- Boolean – a true or false value.

Many programming languages require that variables of different data types are declared (given an initial value) before they are used. Declaration ensures that the required amount of memory is allocated to each variable during the program's execution. Examples of the above data types being declared in the SQA's programming reference language are shown in Figure 3.1.

```
SET score TO 0
SET height TO 194.5
SET name TO "Fred"
SET continueNow TO True
```

Figure 3.1 Data types being declared

Data structures

A structure is used when multiple items of data (for example, the names, addresses and telephone numbers of a thousand customers) are stored. Structures include:

- Arrays – an array consists of numbered elements (storage locations), each of which stores the same data type.

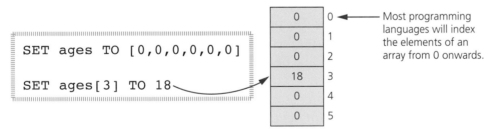

```
SET ages TO [0,0,0,0,0,0]

SET ages[3] TO 18
```

0	0
0	1
0	2
18	3
0	4
0	5

Most programming languages will index the elements of an array from 0 onwards.

Figure 3.2 An array structure and its use

It is common that the elements of an array will be accessed one at a time using repetition (a loop). You must have a good understanding of array use at Higher as all the new standard algorithms make use of arrays.

```
SET allScores TO [7,8,3,5,7,6,7,8,6,5,7,5,5,6,8,3,4,3,5,6]
FOR EACH score FROM allScores DO
    IF score <= 5 THEN SET poorScores TO poorScores + 1
END FOR EACH
SEND "There were" & poorScores & "unacceptable scores" TO DISPLAY
```

Figure 3.3 An example of array use with repetition

- Records – a record is a collection of data stored for one item, person or event. A record may contain a variety of different data types. It is common for programs to be written that read and write data from external databases. Data may be pulled from a record in a database and stored in a similar record structure within the program.
- Sequential files – data may also be written to or read from external files. This is useful if the data is to be kept after the program has executed.

```
RECORD employee IS {STRING name,
    STRING dateOfBirth, INTEGER salary}

employee("John","07/01/1970",32050)
employee("Nicola","24/10/1967",40040)
employee("Myote","01/02/1982",24005)

IF John.salary > Nicola.salary THEN
    SEND "John earns more" TO DISPLAY
END IF
```

Figure 3.4 A record structure and its use

```
OPEN "highScores.txt"
SEND "Greg/n" TO "highScores.txt"
SEND gameScore & "/n" TO "highScore.txt"
CLOSE "highScores.txt"
```

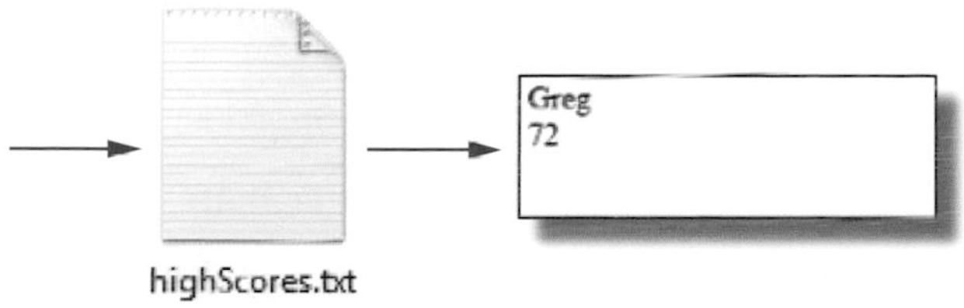

Figure 3.5 Sequential file

Subroutines (sub-programs)

A subroutine is a block of code that has been separated from the main program. Subroutines usually perform a single task or action. The subroutine is 'called' by another part of the program when required, the lines in the subroutine are then executed and the program continues from the call command. Three common types of subroutines are:
- Procedures – these blocks of code perform a task that is contained completely within the procedure's code.
- Functions – the code in a function calculates a value that it returns to the main program.
- Methods – used in object-oriented programming, a method is a subroutine that defines the behaviour of an object.

Modular programming aims to split a program into as many self-contained subroutines as possible. Modularity improves the maintainability of a program as it is possible to re-write a single module without the changes impacting on the rest of the program.

Scope of variables and parameter passing

The scope of a variable refers to in how much of a program's code the variable can be used. A variable may be declared as either:
- Global – these variables can be used throughout a program at any point in the code.
- Local – the values stored in these variables exist within only one part of the code, usually within a subroutine.

The use of local variables allows the same variable name to be used more than once in different parts of a program. This is useful in large programs written by a team, as it means the different programmers don't have to be consistent in the variable names they use.

Modularity and the use of local variables require that some data be passed into a subroutine in order that it may be used locally. Variables created within a subroutine when data is passed are called **parameters**. Variables may be passed into a subroutine by value or by reference.

- Value – if a variable is passed by value, a copy of the data is made within the subroutine. Any changes made to the passed data will not affect the original data. Passing a variable by value requires additional resources as additional memory is required to store the duplicate data.
- Reference – if a variable is passed by reference, the original data is used and modified within the subroutine. No copy of the data is made.

Programming languages may have syntax that allows the programmer to declare if a variable is being passed by value or by reference.

Parameters may be formal or actual

- Formal – this refers to the variable name used within the subroutine to hold the data passed into it, for example, age.
- Actual – this refers to the actual data that is passed into the subroutine, for example, 45.

What you should know

In your revision of this chapter, ensure that you:

- ★ understand the difference between a data type and a data structure
- ★ are able to identify when each type or structure should be used in a given scenario
- ★ can state the advantages of modular programming and the purpose of different subroutines
- ★ can describe the difference between global and local variables
- ★ can identify when a variable should be passed by value or by reference.

Questions

1 A program is required to read a set of light meter readings and dates from a text file. The program will then calculate an average (mean) reading and store a list of dates when the meter readings were within 0.3 of the average. Describe the data types and structures required to implement the program. (4)

2 When most people learn to program they start by writing small programs consisting of a few simple lines of code. Are these initial programs likely to contain global or local variables? Explain your answer. (2)

3 A large program is created where every variable is declared as a global variable. State the effect of two programmers using the same variable name when writing different sections of a large program. (1)

4 A program contains a subroutine that calculates and displays a company's total wage bill. Should the wages of each member of staff be passed into the subroutine by value or by reference? Explain your answer. (2)

5 Some programming languages allow arrays to be passed into a subroutine by reference only. Explain why this restriction may make a program more robust. (2)

Chapter 4
Standard algorithms

Programming involves solving problems by designing algorithms. These solutions are then implemented using a programming language. While some of these algorithms will be unique to a particular problem, others appear regularly in different programs; these are known as standard algorithms.

Once implemented in code, standard algorithms may be saved as **modules**. This saves time later as the code to be reused is already written and tested. A collection of prewritten modules is called a **library**.

The five standard algorithms covered in Higher Computing Science are discussed in turn below. Examples are given using the SQA's reference language. This is the language that will be used in exam questions.

Input validation

Ensuring that data entered into a program by a user is valid ensures that the program does not have to cope with unexpected data. This improves the robustness of a program.

Input validation involves repeatedly asking for input until it meets given criteria. It is good practice to warn the user that they have entered invalid data with a suitable message.

You should already be familiar with input validation from National 5 Computing Science.

```
SEND "Enter a value between 1 and 12." TO DISPLAY
REPEAT
    RECEIVE value FROM (INTEGER) KEYBOARD
    IF value < 1 OR value > 12 THEN
        SEND "Not valid! Enter a value between 1
        and 12." TO DISPLAY
    END IF
UNTIL value >= 1 AND value <= 12
```

Find maximum

The following algorithm finds the largest number in a list of values stored in an array. The algorithm compares each number in the list with a temporary value, and replaces the temporary value if a subsequent number is found to be greater.

```
SET numbers TO [1,56,3,54,26,83,1,5,90,2,5]
SET maxValue TO raceTimes[0]
FOR counter FROM 1 TO length(raceTimes[])
    IF raceTimes[counter] > maxValue THEN
        SET maxValue TO raceTimes[counter]
    END IF
END FOR
SEND ["The maximum race time was " & maxValue] TO
DISPLAY
```

Find minimum

The find minimum algorithm is almost identical to the find maximum algorithm. To find the smallest value in a list, you simply swap the 'greater than' symbol for a 'less than' symbol.

```
SET earthquakeReadings TO [3.4,6.3,2.9,7.6,5.5,1.8,4.2]
SET minValue TO earthquakeReadings[0]
FOR counter FROM 1 TO length(earthquakeReadings[])
    IF earthquakeReadings[counter] < minValue THEN
        SET minValue TO earthquakeReadings[counter]
    END IF
END FOR
SEND ["The smallest magnitude earthquake was " & minValue] TO DISPLAY
```

Linear search

A linear search algorithm examines each value in a list, from first to last. This algorithm could be used to determine whether or not a value can be found in a list, or to search for and display specified values. The example below examines a list of temperatures and displays each value that falls between 10 and 20 as it finds it.

```
SET temperatures TO [9.65,4.77,12.89,19.99,10,23.33,34.26]
SEND "The values found are listed below:" TO DISPLAY
FOR counter FROM 0 TO length(temperatures[])
    IF temperatures [counter] >= 10 AND temperatures [counter] <= 20 THEN
        SEND temperatures [counter] TO DISPLAY
    END IF
END FOR
```

Count occurrences

A count occurrences algorithm displays the number of times that a value occurs in a list. This algorithm is based on the linear search algorithm in that both examine each value in the list.

```
SET weights TO [12,6,34,34,23,19,17,15,9,56,43]
SET totalFound TO 0
FOR counter FROM 0 TO length(weights[])
    IF weights[counter] >= 15 AND weights[counter] <= 18 THEN
        SET totalFound TO totalFound + 1
    END IF
END FOR
SEND ["The number of weights found between 15 and 18 was " & totalFound]
TO DISPLAY
```

What you should know

In your revision of this chapter, ensure that you are able to:
★ explain the purpose of each of the five standard algorithms
★ write out each algorithm from memory in a programming language or in pseudocode
★ adapt each algorithm to suit a given scenario.

Questions

1 State which of the five standard algorithms would have been used to solve the following problems.
   a) A program is written to find a short music track for use in an advert. When a CD is inserted into the computer, the program analyses it and stores the length of each track in seconds. The program then displays the number of tracks that are less than 120 seconds long. (1)
   b) A mobile phone app uses GPS to track the movement of a skier coming down a mountain. The movements are used to record the speed of the skier each second. When the skier stops moving, the app displays the fastest and slowest speeds of their descent down the mountain. (2)
   c) An update for the above skiing app is released, which records only those speeds that are greater than 10mph. When the skier's descent is complete the app now displays all the speeds recorded that were above 30mph. (2)
2 The find maximum algorithm shown in this chapter (page 8) uses the variable maxValue to store and display the maximum number in an array of integers. If this code were implemented, state all the values that would be stored by the variable maxValue during execution. (1)
3 The count occurrences example (page 9) counts the number of weights between 15 and 18. Describe how you would adapt this algorithm to allow the user to select their own lower and upper values. (2)

## Chapter 5

Testing and debugging programs

The purpose of testing a program is to identify errors in the code. Comprehensive testing of a program should focus on whether or not:

- the program meets the requirements as specified in the analysis of the project
- the program responds correctly to input
- data is processed as required and calculations are performed correctly
- the program processes data in an acceptable period of time
- the program produces the required output
- the program has a useable interface
- the program runs correctly in its proper environment.

It is impossible to fully test most software as there may be an almost infinite number of possible inputs. A comprehensive test plan should document a systematic approach to finding as many faults in the software as possible.

Errors in program code

Testing aims to identify errors in program code in order to correct them. Errors in code may include:

- Syntax errors – each programming language has its own set of rules regarding how each instruction must be written or formatted. If these rules are broken a syntax error is created that will prevent the instruction being executed.
- Execution errors – this is an error that occurs while the program is running. Execution errors may involve an attempt to use a variable that has not been declared, use of invalid data, an attempt to access a file that doesn't exist or division by 0.
- Logic errors – a logic error occurs when the code executes but produces the wrong result. Common errors may include AND instead of OR, < instead of >, code written in the wrong order or loops which repeat the wrong number of times.

Types and methods of testing

A **dry run** is an example of **static testing**, a form of testing that involves reading the program code and mentally 'walking through' it without actually running the program. The tester will predict what the code will produce and fix errors before the code is executed. Some static testing is provided by programming tools such as text editors, which highlight errors in syntax.

Dynamic testing is when the code is executed using a set of test data. This may involve the use of a **trace table**, which lists the variables in a program and tracks the values they store as the code is executed.

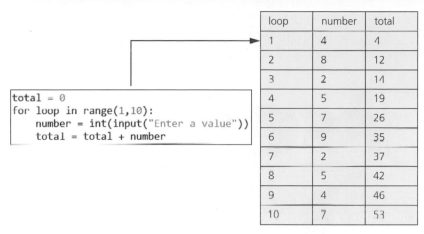

loop	number	total
1	4	4
2	8	12
3	2	14
4	5	19
5	7	26
6	9	35
7	2	37
8	5	42
9	4	46
10	7	53

```
total = 0
for loop in range(1,10):
    number = int(input("Enter a value"))
    total = total + number
```

Figure 5.1 A trace table

A trace table may be used in conjunction with **breakpoints**, which force executing code to pause at given points, thus allowing the current values of variables to be examined.

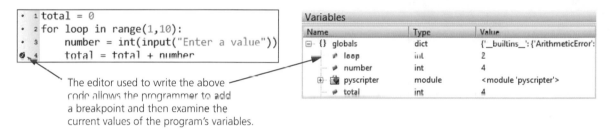

The editor used to write the above code allows the programmer to add a breakpoint and then examine the current values of the program's variables.

Figure 5.2 A breakpoint

Dynamic testing may occur continually during the writing of a program by testing components such as sub-programs, the integration of sub-programs, interfaces and the completed system.

A **test plan** for a small program, such as a Higher Computing Science task, may include dynamic testing that simply checks the program copes with a variety of different inputs:

- Normal – expected data.
- Extreme – data on the limits of expected data.
- Exceptional – unexpected data.

Test plans for large commercial projects will include strategies for each of the following types of testing:

- Functional testing – tests that check if particular features work.
- Alpha testing – tests performed on completed software at the developer's site.
- Beta testing – tests performed offsite by users outside the programming team.
- Acceptance testing – tests performed by the customer in their own environment using their own hardware.
- Compatibility testing – tests that check the software's compatibility with other applications or operating systems.
- Installation testing – tests that ensure the software installs correctly on the customer's hardware.

- Usability testing – tests that check the usability of the user interface.
- Accessibility testing – checks that the software is compatible with disability legislation.

Figure 5.3 Installing software on an office computer

 What you should know

In your revision of this chapter, ensure that you are able to:

★ explain the reasons for testing software
★ describe how software is tested
★ outline the purpose of a test plan
★ identify different types of error in code
★ describe different methods used to test software and find errors in the program's code.

 Questions

1 An app is produced that can be used by cooks to time how long an egg has been boiling. One cook discovers that all her eggs are overcooked because the timer on the app runs more slowly than it should. Explain why this issue should have been identified as part of a comprehensive test plan. (1)
2 State why many programs can never be fully tested. (1)
3 A program crashes following an attempt to divide a value by 0. State the type of error that has occurred. (1)
4 A program module is written to receive and validate a date of birth entered by a user using a keyboard. The user is asked to enter the day, month and year separately. Describe a set of test data that could be used to check that the module is correctly validating the month entered by the user. (3)
5 Explain the difference between static and dynamic testing. (2)

Most programming languages contain instructions that allow the program code to access data held in other files. Without this ability all the data used by a program would have to be stored in the code, entered by the user or received from an external device. The ability to use external files ensures that data can be saved when the program is not running and/or that data can be shared with other programs.

Programs may access a variety of file types, including text, csv and database files. Scripting code, embedded in an HTML file, to access a database is a common example of file handling.

Pseudocode example

In the example below data stored in an array is written to a text file called 'states'. The SQA code shows the file being opened, a loop in which each item in an array is written into the file, and the file being closed.

```
SET stateList TO ["Florida","California","Texas"]
OPEN FILE "states"
FOR EACH oneState FROM stateList DO
    SEND oneState TO states
END FOR EACH
CLOSE FILE "states"
```

Program code example

A bit more information is required in code than in the SQA's reference language. The program code will include:
- an instruction to open the file (creating a connection with the file)
- a path to the file (determined by where the file is saved in relation to the program file)
- syntax to determine whether connection to the file will be read only, write only or read/write
- an instruction to close the file (breaking the connection to the external data).

The code below shows the code above being implemented in the Python programming language.

```
stateList = ["Florida","California","Texas"]
file = open("states.txt","w")
for counter in range(len(stateList)):
    file.write(stateList[counter]+"\n")
file.close()
```

Figure 6.1 The reference language example being implemented in the Python programming language

15

Additional instructions allow a programmer to carry out a variety of other tasks, including creating a new file, deleting a file or deleting the contents of a file.

What you should know

In your revision of this chapter, ensure that you are able to:

★ explain the importance of file handling
★ show an understanding of how a file is accessed and used by a program
★ write simple file handling programs in a programming language of your choice.

Questions

1 A program is required to store five race times (in seconds) entered by a user in a plain text file. In pseudocode or a programming language of your choice, write a short program that will write the five race times to a file called 'raceTimes'. (5)

2 A good programmer should be able to use their knowledge of code to examine the purpose of instructions in unfamiliar languages. Examine the following Python instruction and state the name of the file being accessed, the file type and the type of connection being opened to the file. (3)

```
file = open("mywork/name.txt","r")
```

3 If you are unfamiliar with Python, write a line of code in a programming language with which you are familiar that carries out the task in Question 2. (1)

## Chapter 7

The software development process

The software development process (also known as 'the waterfall model') is a traditional development methodology used when creating new software. It is based on the engineering principle of design and then build. There are seven stages in the process, each of which is treated as an individual project. Although the process has a clear beginning and end it is common to return to earlier stages of the process. This is known as **iteration**.

The seven stages of the software development process are described below.

1 Analysis

The purpose of analysis is to define a problem and the boundaries of the solution to that problem. When creating software a **software specification** will be produced that clearly outlines the features and functions of the program. The specification is produced through discussion between the client and a systems analyst from the software company. The systems analyst may gather additional data such as forms, invoices and paper records used by the client. The specification may be used as a legal contract between the client and the software company. This would be referred to if there were any disagreement regarding the scope of the final product.

2 Design

Before any code is written, a program design is created using a **top-down** approach, which breaks the whole problem down into smaller and smaller sub-problems. The design stage will involve the systems analyst and the project manager.

A variety of design notations may be used, including pseudocode, structure diagrams and wire frames.

Pseudocode

This top-down methodology uses English-like statements to describe how a problem will be solved. The design begins with the drafting of an algorithm (the main steps required to solve the problem), which is then refined by explaining each step in more and more detail if required. If the top-down refinement of the algorithm is comprehensive then each line of pseudocode will equate to one program instruction.

```
Line 1    SET totalRunningTime TO 0
Line 2    <Get valid numberOfTracks from user>
Line 3    FOR counter FROM 1 TO numberOfTracks  DO
Line 4       <Get title and length from user>
Line 5          SET totalRunningTime TO totalRunningTime + trackLength[counter]
Line 6    END FOR
Line 7    <display track titles and track lengths>
Line 8    SEND ["CD-R running time        " & totalRunningTime] TO DISPLAY

Line 2.1    REPEAT
Line 2.2         RECEIVE numberOfTracks  FROM (INTEGER) KEYBOARD
Line 2.3         IF numberOfTracks  < 1 OR numberOfTracks  > 20 THEN
Line 2.4            SEND "Please enter number of tracks between 1 and 20" TO DISPLAY
Line 2.5         END IF
Line 2.6    UNTIL numberOfTracks >= 1 AND numberOfTracks <= 20

Line 4.1    RECEIVE trackTitle[counter]  FROM (STRING) KEYBOARD
Line 4.2    RECEIVE trackLength[counter]  FROM (REAL) KEYBOARD

Line 7.1    FOR counter FROM 1 TO numberOfTracks  DO
Line 7.2         SEND [trackTitle[counter] & trackLength[counter]] TO DISPLAY
Line 7.3    END FOR
```

Figure 7.1 An example of a pseudocode design

Structure diagram

A structure diagram is another top-down methodology. This represents all the different elements that must be present in the software as hierarchical blocks. The lines on the diagram below show how the structure is refined.

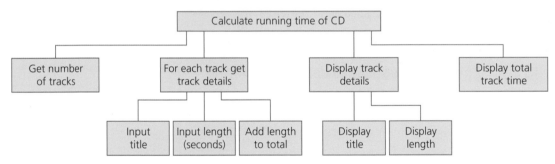

Figure 7.2 An example of a structure diagram design

Wire frames

Wire frames are formalised sketches of screen layouts. In software development they are often used to design user interface screens. More information on wire framing and their use in designing web pages may be found in Chapter 13.

It is common for the design stage to take as long as the implementation stage that follows. A good clear design can ensure fewer errors during implementation and testing.

3 Implementation

The design is implemented by writing the program. The programming language that is used will be determined by:

- the specific problem, as different languages have different attributes that make them suited to web-based, mathematical, database, communication or graphical problems
- the type of user interface required
- the experience of the programmers.

Smaller programs may be written by a single programmer, but with larger programs the project manager will allocate individual tasks (user interface, sound, database integration, etc.) to different programmers according to their skill set.

4 Testing

Testing occurs in distinct phases throughout the software development process. While code is being written, each small part will be tested to ensure it executes without crashing. When the code is complete, the whole program will be tested in-house in a process called **alpha** testing. After that, **beta** testing takes place – this is where the software is tested externally by individuals not involved in the creation of the software. The individuals may be contracted specialists. Finally, the software is tested on the customer's own hardware, known as **acceptance** testing.

5 Documentation

The purpose of this stage is to produce documentation that will be distributed with the program. Two common documents are:
- the **user guide**, which explains how to use the features of the program
- the **technical guide**, which includes the minimum hardware specification required to use the program and details of how to install/ set up the software.

The production of useful, accurate documentation will rely on input from the client, the systems analyst and the programmers.

6 Evaluation

The software company will evaluate the success of each project. The identification of mistakes made may ensure that the next project is completed faster and with fewer errors, which would increase the software company's profits.

Evaluation of the software itself may identify efficiency savings that could have been made in coding or resource allocation such as memory usage. Again, this information may be of use in future projects.

7 Maintenance

Once software is complete it is common to return at a later date to change or update the software. There are three types of maintenance carried out by software companies:
- Perfective – new features are added to the software to improve (perfect) it.
- Corrective – bugs or errors discovered after completion of the software are fixed (corrected).
- Adaptive – the software must be altered (adapted) due to an external influence, such as a change to the operating system on which the software runs.

Increased download speeds – resulting from the introduction of broadband, 3G and 4G telecommunications – have improved the ease with which updates to software can be installed. Maintenance of software is consequently now commonplace, with updates to games and apps appearing regularly.

Rapid Application Development

Rapid Application Development (RAD) challenges the traditional view of software development. It recognises that the solution used to solve a problem changes as knowledge is gained during the production process. This therefore suggests that spending too much time on an initial design is a waste as the design will constantly change. RAD aims to take advantage of the knowledge gained during production and use it to change the solution for the better.

RAD projects involve the development of small, quickly built prototypes. This reduces risk as the different parts of the software can be tested sooner, identifying potential problems. The client can be shown working components of the software, allowing them to give feedback and suggest changes. In the traditional method, in contrast, the client would not see the software until a complete working version was implemented late in the process. This may be too late for the client to change their mind or suggest possible improvements. Once a prototype is accepted it can be used to build the finished component.

Agile methodologies

The introduction of RAD in the 1980s led to the growth of a variety of agile methodologies. Agile principles aim to improve customer satisfaction by delivering software in weeks rather than in months. Small, motivated project teams are formed in single locations, nicknamed 'bullpens'. The project group contains a variety of skills and each group relies on face-to-face conversation to make quick decisions. This vastly improves the developer's ability to react should the client's requirements change. The success of a project is measured by the speed at which completed software is produced.

There are a few known disadvantages of agile methodologies:
- The types of decisions made by the project groups require experience. Agile development is not suited to new programmers unless they are very well supported.
- The lack of emphasis on design and documentation may cause problems.
- The lack of stringent design at the beginning of a project may make it difficult to predict the timescale of the project.
- If the client representative who is working with the project group is not clear about their requirements then the project may be easily taken in the wrong direction.

What you should know

In your revision of this chapter, ensure that you are able to:
* write a definition of each stage of the software development process
* describe the documents created during the different stages of the software development process
* describe the roles of the different personnel involved in the software development process
* describe RAD, including its advantages and disadvantages
* describe agile methodologies, including their advantages and disadvantages.

Questions

1 State an example of iteration in the software development process. (1)
2 Explain why the lack of emphasis on documentation occasionally found while using agile methodologies may make maintenance of software more difficult. (1)
3 A user reports that following an upgrade to their database their application is now failing to connect to the upgraded database. State the type of maintenance that the application requires. (1)
4 Explain why wire frames are suitable only to design user interfaces and not actual code. (1)
5 State two advantages to the client of a developer using agile methodologies to develop software. (2)
6 State why the software development process (the waterfall method) is rarely used in modern software production. (1)
7 Describe one situation where perfective maintenance may be carried out on a mobile phone app. (1)

## Chapter 8

Data representation

Why use binary?

At its lowest level a computer system consists of microscopic switches called transistors. Transistors are used in computer circuitry to store and process data such as numbers, text, graphics, sound and video. A switch has only two states (on and off), meaning that all the data stored and processed by a computer system is represented using binary values that comprise the digits 0 (off) and 1 (on).

The design, manufacture and use of a computer system based around the binary counting system, rather than the denary counting system, has several advantages:

- The mathematical rules of binary are simple. When adding two binary digits, for example, there are only four possible combinations, 0+0, 0+1, 1+0 and 1+1. This makes computer circuitry easier to design and build.
- The computer system is not affected by voltage fluctuations. If we built a computer based on denary (our counting system using the numbers 0 to 9), we could have different voltages representing different values (1V=1, 2V=2, and so on). Voltages in circuits tend to fluctuate. If the voltage in the circuitry experienced a brief spike and 2V became 2.7V, this may corrupt the data in the computer as the value 2 may in this case be regarded as a 3. In a binary computer system, where there are only two states (say 0V=0 and 5V=1), a small change in voltage would have no effect on the values stored.
- It is easier to design and manufacture storage devices (disk drives, optical drives, solid state drives) that store data using only two states.

Storing numbers

Many programming languages require that when a numeric variable is declared, the programmer must note in the code if an integer or a real number is being stored. This is because each data type has different storage requirements.

Integers (whole numbers) are stored using simple binary numbers as shown below.

128	64	32	16	8	4	2	U	
1	1	1	0	1	1	0	1	= 128+64+32+8+4+1 = 237

Figure 8.1 Integers stored using simple binary numbers

Integers are commonly stored as 8, 16, 32, 64 or 128 bit binary numbers.

Although there are several methods used by computer systems to store negative integers, the most commonly used notation is **two's**

complement. In this method, the left-most bit is used to store the negative equivalent of that column, as shown below.

-128	64	32	16	8	4	2	U
1	1	1	0	1	1	0	1

$= -128+64+32+8+4+1 = -19$

Figure 8.2 Negative integers stored using simple binary numbers

Real numbers (numbers with decimal places) are stored using floating point notation, as shown below.

For example, the number 345765000 would be stored as:

$$3.45765 \times 10^8$$

The computer then stores two separate integers with a set number of bits.

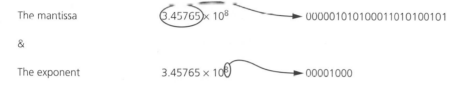

The mantissa   3.45765 × 10⁸ ⟶ 00000101010100011010100101

&

The exponent   3.45765 × 10⁸ ⟶ 00001000

Figure 8.3 Real numbers stored using floating point notation

Note that the mantissa and exponent may also be stored using two's complement, thus allowing negative values to be stored. Real numbers may also vary in size (32, 64 and 80 bits are common). If 32 bits are used, 24 bits may be allocated to the mantissa while the remaining 8 bits would be the exponent part of the number.

Storing text

Text is stored by using a binary number code to represent each character. The American Standard Code for Information Interchange (**ASCII**) is an 8-bit code used to store 256 different text characters. The ASCII code is limited to storing some control characters, numbers, the alphabet used in English and a selection of characters from other languages (e.g. accents such as ú, ó, é). **Unicode** is a 16-bit code capable of storing 65 536 different characters, numbers and symbols. A sample of the type of data stored by ASCII and by Unicode is shown below.

ASCII

6	00110110 (54)	W	00110111 (87)
7	00110111 (55)	X	00111000 (88)
8	00111000 (56)	Y	00111001 (89)
9	00111001 (57)	Z	00111010 (90)
:	00111010 (58)	[	00111011 (91)
;	00111011 (59)	/	00111100 (92)
<	00111100 (60)	]	00111101 (93)
=	00111101 (61)	^	00111110 (94)
>	00111110 (62)	_	00111111 (95)
?	00111111 (63)	`	00110000 (96)
@	00100000 (64)	a	00110001 (97)

Figure 8.4 ASCII and Unicode

Unicode

Greek and Coptic
Official Unicode Consortium code chart

	0	1	2	3	4	5	6	7	8	9	A	B	C	D	E	F
U+037x	Ͱ	ͱ	Ͳ	ͳ	ʹ	͵	Ͷ	ͷ				ͺ	;		;	Ϳ
U+038x				΄	΅	Ά	·	Έ	Ή	Ί		Ό		Ύ	Ώ
U+039x	ΐ	Α	Β	Γ	Δ	Ε	Ζ	Η	Θ	Ι	Κ	Λ	Μ	Ν	Ξ	Ο
U+03Ax	Π	Ρ		Σ	Τ	Υ	Φ	Χ	Ψ	Ω	Ϊ	Ϋ	ά	έ	ή	ί
U+03Bx	ΰ	α	β	γ	δ	ε	ζ	η	θ	ι	κ	λ	μ	ν	ξ	ο
U+03Cx	π	ρ	ς	σ	τ	υ	φ	χ	ψ	ω	ϊ	ϋ	ό	ύ	ώ	Ϗ
U+03Dx	ϐ	ϑ	ϒ	ϓ	ϔ	ϕ	ϖ	ϗ	Ϙ	ϙ	Ϛ	ϛ	Ϝ	ϝ	Ϟ	ϟ
U+03Ex	Ϡ	ϡ	Ϣ	ϣ	Ϥ	ϥ	Ϧ	ϧ	Ϩ	ϩ	Ϫ	ϫ	Ϭ	ϭ	Ϯ	ϯ
U+03Fx	ϰ	ϱ	ϲ	ϳ	ϴ	ϵ	϶	Ϸ	ϸ	Ϲ	Ϻ	ϻ	ϼ	Ͻ	Ͼ	Ͽ

Storing graphics

Graphics may be stored as either bit-mapped or vector graphics.

A **bit-mapped graphic** comprises rows and columns of coloured pixels, as shown below.

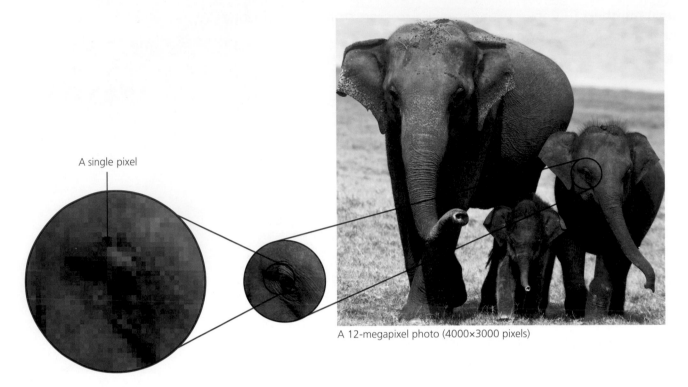

A single pixel

A 12-megapixel photo (4000×3000 pixels)

Figure 8.5 Bit-mapped graphic

Each pixel is stored as a binary number with the number of possible colours in a bit-mapped graphic being determined by the number of bits used to store each pixel. This is known as its **colour depth**.

- 8 bits = 2^8 = 256 possible colours
- 16 bits = 2^{16} = 65 536 possible colours
- 24 bit colour ('true' colour) is often stored in the red, green, blue (rgb) format, where each colour is an 8 bit number from 0 to 255.

The storage requirements for an uncompressed bit-mapped graphic can be calculated as:

Size of graphic file = Resolution (number of pixels) × Colour depth (the number of bits used to store each pixel)

A **vector graphic** is created from shapes, as shown below.

Figure 8.6 Vector graphic

Regular shapes (polygons, ellipses, text) are stored by saving a list of attributes for the shape: x and y co-ordinates, length, width, fill colour, line thickness and so on.

Irregular shapes are created in a vector graphics application by manipulating a series of nodes and curves. The angles at which the curves enter and leave each node create the outline of the shape and are altered by moving handles attached to each curve. The outline of an irregular shape is stored by saving the position of these nodes and the angle of each curve. The remaining attributes are stored as for a regular shape.

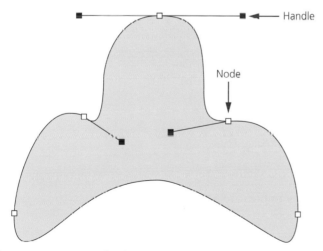

Figure 8.7 Vector graphic for an irregular shape

Storing sound

To store sound as digital data, an analogue sound must be converted into a series of binary values. This is achieved by taking regular 'samples' of single points on the wave and converting the amplitude of the wave at each point into a binary number. A stereo sound with left and right channels will store samples for two waves.

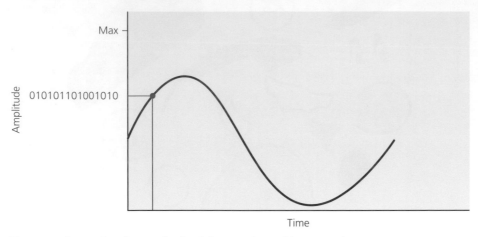

Figure 8.8 Converting the amplitude of the wave into a binary number

The sound quality of a digitised sound is determined by:
- sample rate – how often a sample is taken
- sample depth – this determines the number of different values that may be used to store the amplitude of the wave.

With a high quality sound the steps in the digital wave may be so small (due to very high sample rate and depth) that the wave will closely resemble the original analogue wave. A low sampling rate and depth will result in poor quality sound as the digital wave will have large steps between each sampled point.

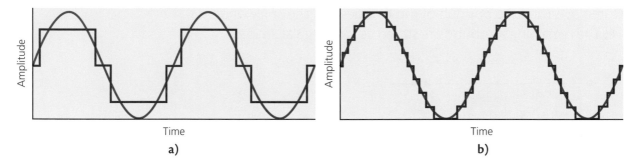

Figure 8.9 a) Low sampling rate and depth, and **b)** high sampling rate and depth

The storage requirements for a sound file can be calculated using this formula:

Size of sound file = Number of channels × Sample depth × Sample rate × Time (seconds)

Storing video

Uncompressed videos are stored as a sequence of still bit-mapped graphics. The number of still graphics stored is determined by the frame rate (the number of frames or images displayed each second) and the length of the video (in seconds).

 × number of still images

Figure 8.10 Video frames

The storage requirements for a video file can be calculated using this formula:

Size of video file = Resolution × Colour depth × Frame rate × Time (secs)

Uncompressed video files are fairly rare because the file sizes can be very large.

Compression

A file is compressed (reduced in size) by applying one or more compression techniques. The storage of compressed bit mapped graphics, vector graphics, sound and video files will be covered in Chapter 15.

What you should know 👍

In your revision of this chapter, ensure that you are able to:

★ explain fully how text, graphics, sound and video are stored using binary
★ explain the effect on file size when one or more of the attributes of a file changes, for example when the resolution increases in a bit-mapped graphic or when a sound file is changed from stereo to mono
★ explain how the term 'quality' relates to the different attributes of a file, for example, that a high-quality video will have a high resolution and frame rate
★ calculate the file size of each uncompressed file type
★ explain the difference between a compressed and an uncompressed file.

Questions ?

1 Explain why a computer system's CPU stores and processes data in binary form. (1)

2 Explain why it would be inefficient for a computer to store every numeric value using floating point notation. (1)

3 State the binary equivalent of the value 328. (1)

4 State the range of numbers that can be expressed in 8 bits using two's complement notation. (2)

5 State the two's complement 8-bit binary number equivalent of -212. (1)

6 Assuming the number is stored using two's complement notation, calculate the denary number represented by the 10-bit binary number 1001010010. (1)

7 State a limitation of ASCII code compared to Unicode when storing text. (1)

8 Calculate the storage requirements of a 24-bit colour graphic with a resolution of 3000 × 2400. (2)

9 Look carefully at the following svg (scalable vector graphic) code for a rectangle.
State the colour depth of the rectangle when the vector graphic is displayed. (1)

```
<svg>
<rect width="200" height="200"
fill="rgb(234,255,234)" stroke-width="1"
stroke="rgb(23,0,0)"/>
</svg>
```

10 A sound is sampled with a sampling depth of 16 bits. State the number of different values that may be used to represent the amplitude of the wave at each sampled point. (1)

11 Calculate the file size of a video with the following attributes:
resolution = 1920 × 1080, 16-bit colour depth, 20 fps, 3 mins long. (2)

## Chapter 9

Low level operations and structure

Computer architecture

The purpose of a computer system is to process instructions in order to carry out a task. Although there have been significant developments in hardware complexity and processing speed, computer systems are still based on the architecture developed by mathematician John von Neumann in the 1940s.

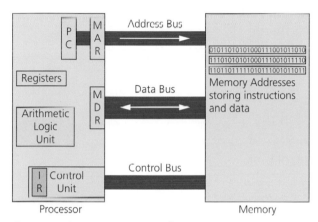

Figure 9.1 Computer system architecture

Fetch execute cycle

A program (list of instructions) is loaded into the memory addresses of the computer system memory. Buses are used to carry instructions, data and signals between the memory and the processor where the instructions are executed.

Programs are executed (or run) by following the **fetch execute cycle** steps below:

1   The memory address of the next instruction to be fetched is placed in the memory address register (MAR).
2   The read line of the control bus is activated by the control unit.
3   The instruction is located at the memory address specified by the address bus and is sent along the data bus to the memory data register.
4   The instruction is transferred to the instruction register, where it is decoded and executed.

Inside the processor

During the execution of an instruction, the **arithmetic logic unit** (ALU) may be required to carry out calculations or make logical decisions such as comparing two values.

The **registers** are used if the instruction requires that data be temporarily stored while being processed. Some registers are for general use while others have a specific role. For example, the program counter stores the address of the next instruction to be fetched.

The **control unit** is responsible for overseeing all operations within the processor. These include:

- Timing each event using the computer system's clock.
- Initiating the transfer of data along the data bus by activating the read and write lines of the control bus.
- Interrupting the processor if another task (process) needs to be dealt with.
- Telling the ALU how to respond to various instructions.

Memory read and memory write operations

Data may be read from memory into the processor to be used, or it may be written from the processor to be stored in memory. Read/write operations are similar to the fetch execute cycle but do not involve executing an instruction.

Memory read operation:

1 The memory address of the data to be fetched is placed in the memory address register (MAR).
2 The read line on the control bus is activated by the control unit.
3 The data is located at the memory address specified by the address bus and is sent along the data bus to the memory data register.

Memory write operation:

1 The memory address of the data to be fetched is placed in the memory address register (MAR).
2 The data to be written is placed in the memory data register (MDR).
3 The write line on the control bus is activated by the control unit.
4 The data is sent along the data bus and stored in the memory address specified by the address bus.

Development trends

As stated earlier, central processing unit (CPU) technology has developed significantly since von Neumann's original design.

- **Buses** have been widened to allow for increased memory addresses on computer systems and for more data to be stored at each address. Note that the maximum amount of memory that may be installed on a computer is set by the number of possible addresses (the width of the address bus, AB) multiplied by the size of each address (the width of the data bus, DB).

  $$\text{Max memory} = 2^{AB} \times DB$$

- **Multicore processors** allow more than one instruction to be processed simultaneously. This allows multicore processors to effectively run more than one program simultaneously. For example, running a javascript program on a web page while playing an embedded video.

- Faster types of memory are used to predict and store the next instructions to be executed. This **cache** memory has wider buses and is located near or within the processor, resulting in extremely fast data transfer rates.

The diagram below shows the complexity of a modern, multicore processor.

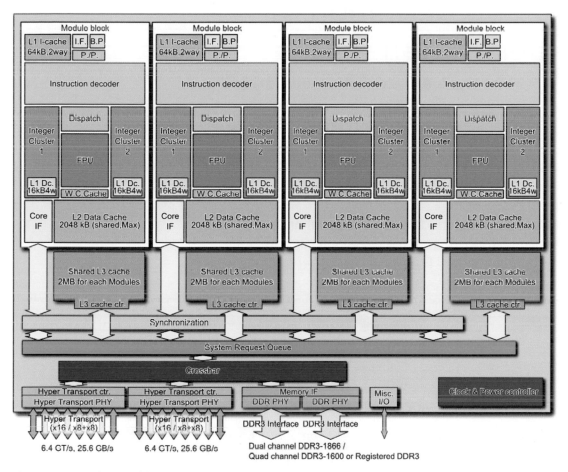

Figure 9.2 A modern, multicore processor

Interfaces

When performing tasks the CPU will often be required to communicate with input, output and backing storage devices. These peripheral devices may:

- work at different voltages to the CPU
- transfer data differently
- use serial transmission
- be analogue devices
- transfer data at different speeds.

The purpose of an interface is to allow the CPU to communicate with peripheral devices by compensating for these differences. An interface may be involved in:

- converting an analogue signal to a digital value or vice versa
- converting serial transmission (one bit being sent at a time down a single wire) to parallel data (multiple bits being sent down multiple wires simultaneously) for transfer down an internal bus

- temporarily storing data in a buffer until a slower peripheral device is ready to receive it
- using status signals to ask the current state of an external device (busy, ready to receive data, etc.).

The changing definition of a computer system

The traditional view of what a computer system looks like has changed since the 1990s.

- The development of small, powerful, low-power processors has led to the rise of a variety of **mobile devices** such as notebooks, tablets and smartphones. High resolution screens and increased storage capacity means the specification of these devices is equal to that of some desktop and laptop PCs.
- An **emulator** is a program that imitates the behaviour of another computer system. Emulators may be used to test circuits and computer systems before they are built, or may be used to simulate old systems such as games consoles.

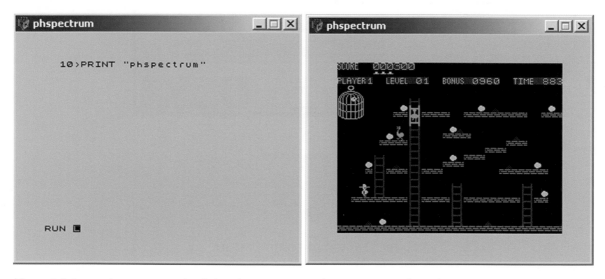

Figure 9.3 An emulator program simulating the ZX Spectrum home computer from the 1980s

- A **virtual machine** is a type of emulator that recreates a complete substitute of a full computer system (hardware and operating system). Figure 9.4 shows an Apple Mac computer running Windows as a virtual machine. This effectively allows the Mac owner to install and run Windows software on their computer. Virtual machines may be cloud-based, running as a remote window on the user's computer system. Cloud-based virtual machines are often purchased on a subscription basis.

Figure 9.4 A Windows virtual machine running on an Apple Mac computer

What you should know

In your revision of this chapter, ensure that you are able to:

★ explain how a computer system stores and processes data and instructions
★ state the function of the CPU's buses
★ describe the functions of the control unit
★ write out, from memory, the fetch execute cycle, memory read and memory write steps
★ discuss recent developments in CPU architecture
★ explain the terms 'mobile device', 'emulator' and 'virtual machine'.

Questions

1 State two differences between the steps required to carry out a memory read operation and a memory write operation. (2)
2 State the role of the ALU, control unit and registers when processing the instruction below. (3)

```
IF num1 > num2 THEN
```

3 A student is recording a jingle for his school's website. Discuss one role of an interface when receiving data from a microphone. (1)
4 Calculate the maximum amount of memory that can be installed on a small motherboard with a 24-bit address bus and a 32-bit data bus. (2)
5 Describe one development in CPU architecture and explain how it has resulted in an increase in processing power. (1)
6 Mairi owns a PC running the Windows operating system. She wishes to write a book using a program called iAuthor, which is available only for Apple Macs. Suggest a solution to Mairi's problem that does not involve purchasing a second computer system. (1)

## Chapter 10

Contemporary developments

Software development language trends

New programming languages are being created all the time. Development may be driven by industry need or result from academic research. Some of the current trends in programming language development include:

- Increased methods of improving security in software.
- Different ways of creating modular code.
- Metaprogramming, in which programs are created to write other programs.
- Extended parallel languages for coding supercomputers with thousands of processors.
- An increase in open source languages created by an online community and distributed for free.
- Languages which improve integration with databases.
- Languages whose source code supports Unicode rather than ASCII.

Software development environment trends

In addition to new languages, new editing environments have improved programmers' productivity by providing better editing, checking and debugging facilities.

A source code editor has features such as indentation, text prediction, bracket matching and syntax highlighting. These features speed up the inputting and editing of source code. Source code editors evolved from simple text editors that behaved as basic word processors. Source code editors now can check syntax while it is being entered, immediately warning the user of potential problems.

Many modern development environments offer both compiler and interpreter translation of code.

A modern debugger will feature a variety of debugging tools, including:

- Single stepping – executing a program one line at a time with each step forward being controlled by the user.
- Breakpoints – stopping execution at identified points.
- Variable tracking – windows showing the current values stored in variables and data structures.

An **integrated development environment** (IDE) is a development environment that combines multiple tools, such as a source code editor, debugger, interpreter and compiler. Modern IDEs may also have the ability to browse objects and classes for use in object-oriented programming.

PyScripter is an IDE used to edit Python code. Python is an open source programming language. The graphic below shows a few of the development environment's facilities.

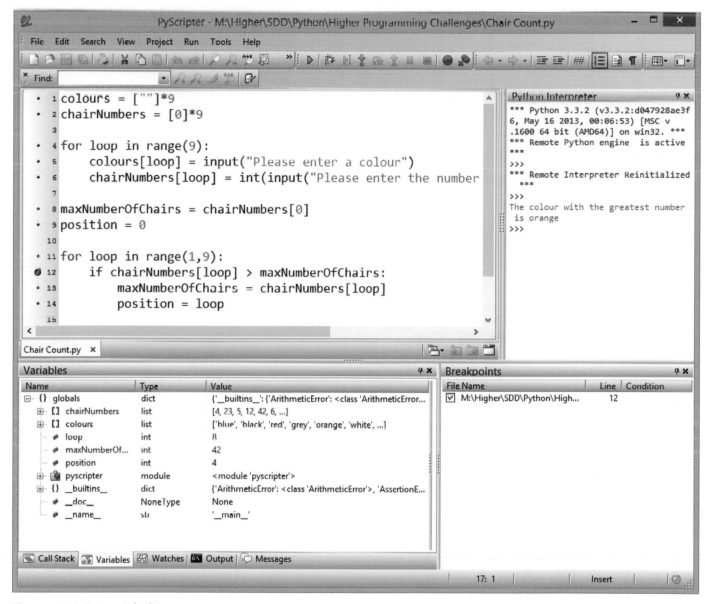

Figure 10.1 PyScripter's facilities

Intelligent systems developments

An intelligent computer is an embedded computer with the ability to communicate with other systems via the internet. These computer systems are usually specialised machines built for a specific purpose.

Examples of intelligent systems are everywhere, from traffic lights to aeroplanes. Some theorists predict that in the future every object and person will be able to share data continuously and automatically, creating an 'Internet of Things'.

Online systems developments

The convergence of database and website technologies has led to a significant rise in systems that are entirely online.

Booking systems now often have no human interaction. Users can log in to websites to book hotel rooms, train tickets, concert tickets and even doctors' appointments. The online system will automatically generate an email in which the user may receive electronic tickets or a booking confirmation. This can be printed as evidence of the online booking. Some systems may take this even further and allow users to confirm their arrival by scanning a barcode or entering a purchase code into a computer system. Online booking systems have significant financial advantages to companies, as with fewer staff, their wage bill may be dramatically reduced, increasing their profits.

Another example of online systems growth is comparison websites. These automated websites analyse the product offers of other websites and collate the information to display the best deals currently available. Again, no human interaction is involved in searching for or collating the information.

Online systems can also have a positive effect on the job market. Significantly more IT staff are required each year to create and maintain the software and hardware required to implement online systems.

What you should know

In your revision of this chapter, ensure that you are able to:

★ discuss contemporary developments in computing
★ state examples of contemporary developments
★ explain the term 'integrated development environment'
★ explain the term 'intelligent systems'
★ state examples of intelligent systems
★ explain the term 'online system'
★ state examples of online systems.

Questions

1   Any user wishing to write code in the programming language Python can download and install numerous free IDEs. Discuss the advantage of using more than one IDE. (1)
2   Many IDEs allow the user to program in more than one language. State why this is an advantage to the user. (1)
3   Describe the purpose of a breakpoint when debugging program code. (2)
4   Modern police cars are fitted with cameras capable of reading the number plate of a car the police car is following. The system can then inform the police officers if the car is not insured. Explain why this is an example of an intelligent system. (2)
5   Explain why an online booking system that allows a customer to search for a hotel room is an example of website and database technologies converging. (1)
6   Describe two economic benefits that may encourage a company to implement an online booking system. (2)

## Chapter 11

SDD unit assessment preparation

Purpose of assessment

All Curriculum for Excellence (CfE) courses are created around **outcomes** and **standards**. Outcomes note what you must be taught in each unit, while the standards supply the details of how each outcome will be covered. The purpose of unit assessments is to gather evidence that each student has met the appropriate standards.

CfE unit assessments are graded as a pass or a fail. There are no marks. To pass the assessment you must pass all the assessment standards listed below.

Outcomes	Assessment standards
1 Explain how programs work, including advanced concepts in software development and computer architecture.	Read and explain code.
	Describe the purpose of a range of programming constructs.
	Describe a range of standard algorithms.
	Describe how programs relate to low-level structures and operations.
2 Develop a program, with subroutines, using one or more software development environments.	Design a program using a contemporary methodology.
	Use a combination of programming constructs.
	Use simple and structured data types (including an array).
	Systematically test your program.
	Correct identified errors.
	Apply good programming techniques (meaningful variable names, internal commentary, indentation)

Conditions of assessment

- Outcome 1 may be assessed through a theory task.
- Outcome 2 will be assessed through a programming task.

It is possible to combine the two outcomes into one task by correctly explaining the purpose of your code using comment lines.

All assessments will take place in class without assistance.

Assessments are 'open book', which means you can refer to any resources (workbooks, tutorials, textbooks, the world wide web) to help you carry out the practical tasks or write up your report.

There is no set time limit for each assessment, but as your teacher has a course to complete it would be unrealistic to assume that you will get as long as you want to complete the tasks and report.

Possible tasks

Outcome 1 could be assessed by asking you to:
- read and explain the purpose of a given piece of code
- describe the purpose of three of the standard algorithms (input validation, linear search, find maximum, find minimum, count occurrences)
- describe how high level language instructions are executed.

You could be given questions to answer, to assess your knowledge of this outcome, or you may be asked to explain code you have written.

For Outcome 2 you will be given a program to:
- design
- implement
- test
- correct.

You will be expected to use good programming practices to ensure your code is readable. At Higher level you should ensure that you are writing modular code using procedures and functions.

Preparation

Any programming task you are given will focus on the additional learning that separates Higher from National 5. This includes reading and writing from files, procedures/functions, parameter passing, object-oriented coding and the standard algorithms. Make sure you practise all of these before you sit the assessment.

Read your theory notes before the assessment, concentrating on the standards listed in Outcomes 1 and 3. Improving your knowledge of these areas of the Higher course will make the tasks of answering the questions and writing your report easier.

Advice

The assessments are not designed to test your memory. Remember that this is an open book assessment. You will have created examples of code as you worked through your school's programming practical work. Make sure that you have labelled these files clearly so that you can open them easily and use them for reference.

Complete each task. This may appear obvious, but many of the assessments that teachers hand back to students to redo have nothing wrong with them, they simply have parts missing. Read the instructions carefully to ensure you haven't missed anything.

Concentrate. If you are too relaxed at the beginning of the task, you will rush the end of it. Your work will lack detail and you may fail one or more standards.

What happens if I fail?

If you fail an outcome or standard you will not be asked to resit the whole assessment. Your teacher will offer you one opportunity to attempt part of the assessment again. Your teacher is allowed to advise you on which standards you have not met but is not allowed to tell you how to fix your mistakes. Between attempts, ensure that you research or practise the parts you did not pass.

If you continue to fail outcomes and standards you will not be allowed to sit the exam at the end of the year. Before you become too worried about this, remember that you are in a Higher class because your teacher thinks you are capable of completing the course.

Unit 2 Information Systems Design and Development

## Chapter 12

Relational database design, implementation and use

Relational database design

Once the purpose of a database has been identified and the appropriate information collected, the structure of the database (tables, fields and relationships) is designed. Designing a large database is a highly specialised job, often carried out by a trained expert. Regular communication between the designer and the end users of the database is necessary to ensure that all the required data is included and that the database performs functions (queries, forms, reports and calculations) as expected.

The most common database design methodology is an **entity relationship diagram** (ER Diagram). Initial drafts of ER Diagrams may be completed informally using pencil and paper, with later versions being produced using specialist ER Diagram software.

Entity relationship diagram basics

The purpose of an ER Diagram is to map out all the database **entities**, their **attributes** and the **relationships** between the entities. The symbols used to represent these are:

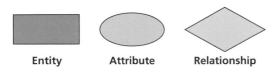

Entity   **Attribute**   **Relationship**

Figure 12.1 Symbols used in ER Diagrams

When connected, the symbols show the data on each entity that will be stored and the relationships between the entities. The diagram below shows part of a database used to store information on films and their actors.

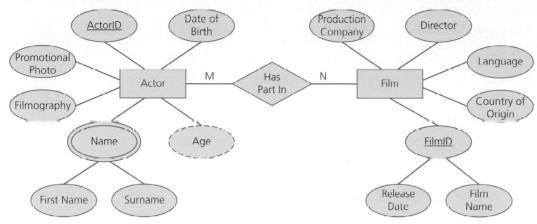

Figure 12.2 A database storing information on films and their actors

Each relationship should show the **cardinality** (the numbers involved in the relationship: one-to-one, one-to-many, many-to-many). There are a few symbols used for cardinality in ER Diagrams to denote 'many': N, M and ∞.

Note that in Figure 12.2:

- The **primary key** ActorID is shown by underlining the name of the attribute.
- The primary key FilmID is also shown by underlining the attribute name. The diagram additionally shows that this is a **compound key**, a unique key made by combining the two attributes 'Film Name' and 'Release Date'.
- Attributes that could store multiple values are indicated using a double line. For example, an Actor may have two names, their given name and their stage name.
- Attributes that can be derived from other attributes have a dotted line. In the diagram, Age can be calculated from the Date of Birth attribute.
- Director and Production Company are attributes of each Film. These could easily be entities in their own rights, each with their own set of attributes. The database designer and users would determine the extent of the data to be stored in the database, thus determining the size of the final ER Diagram.

ER Diagram notations

Over the years, many different ways of drawing ER Diagrams have developed. Some use different symbols while others show the entities and attributes as tables. The notation used in this book is Chen's notation. Don't worry if your teacher has used a different notation as it will still contain the same information.

Refining an entity relationship diagram

Once all the required entities and their relationships have been drawn on the ER Diagram, a designer will apply **normalisation** principles to improve the design. The purpose of normalisation is to minimise redundancy (the same field(s) being present in more than one table) so that data can be inserted, deleted and modified in just one table. In an ER Diagram this is usually achieved by the insertion of further entities and relationships into the diagram.

Many-to-many relationships should be expanded to produce two one-to-many relationships. This is because many-to-many relationships almost always conceal a hidden entity. As the purpose of an ER Diagram is to identify identities and relationships, it's important that the missing entity is added.

Data dictionary (database)

A data dictionary lists all the files in the database, including the number of records, the names of fields and the types of each field. The dictionary is used by database management systems as it defines the basic organisation of each database. Note that data dictionaries are used to manage the database only and do not contain any of the actual data stored in the database.

Relational database operations

Databases are created for the purpose of organising, extracting and presenting the information stored in them. This is done using forms, queries and reports.

A **form** is a layout used to enter data into database tables. The form may contain fields from one or more tables, allowing multiple tables to be updated at once. Forms can be used to create a user interface for a database, whereby the user can add information without any knowledge of how the data is stored and organised. Where a form is embedded in a document (such as a web page) a scripting language is required to pass the data to the database.

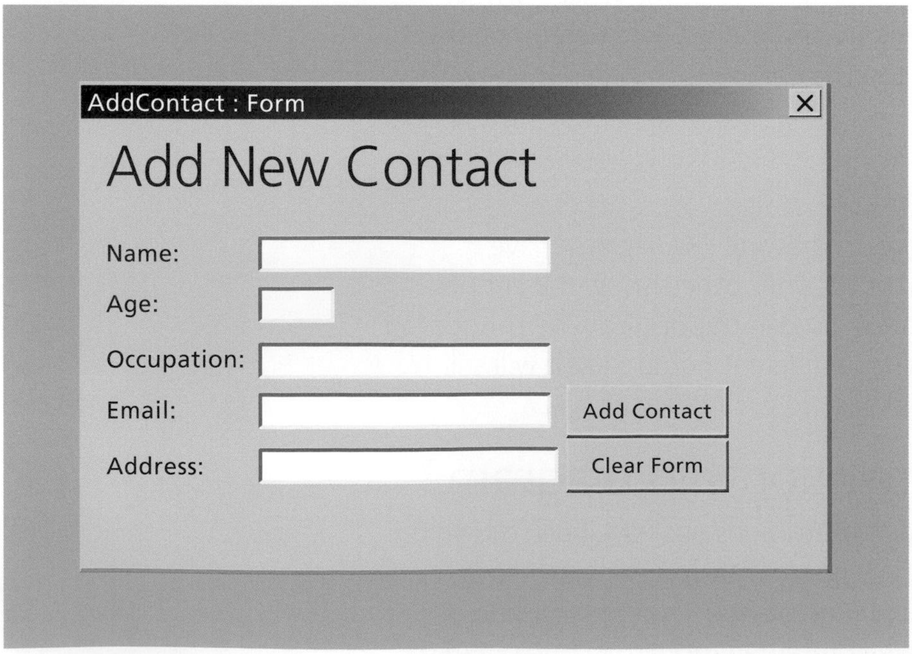

Figure 12.3 A form

A **query** is a set of instructions that searches one or more database tables using entered criteria. When executed, the query will return appropriate results. While database applications like MS Access and FileMaker Pro provide graphical interfaces to build queries, a database may also be queried using a special purpose programming language, such as Structured Query Language (SQL).

SQL instructions are often embedded in other host languages such as PHP, Python, Visual Basic or C. The host language sends the SQL instruction to Database Management Software (DBMS), which processes the instruction. If the instruction is a query the results will be returned and dealt with by the host language.

EmployeeID	Forename	Surname	Age
1013646	Matthew	Reid	23
1020089	George	Coltart	47

JobID	EmployeeID	Hours Taken
12	1013646	5.5
13	1020089	19
14	1010478	8.25
15	1020062	20

Figure 12.4 Database tables: Employees (top) and Jobs (bottom)

Basic SQL instructions (using the above example tables in Figure 12.4):
- SELECT enables you to select every column (*) or chosen columns from one or more tables:

```
SELECT * FROM Employees;
```

- If your database field or table names contain a space, the name should be enclosed in [] brackets:

```
SELECT JobID, [Hours Taken] FROM Jobs;
```

- The selection can contain search criteria using the WHERE command:

```
SELECT JobID FROM Jobs WHERE [Hours Taken] > 10;
```

- Operators like AND, OR and NOT may also be used. The ORDER command sorts the selected data:

```
SELECT Forename, Surname, JobID
FROM Employees, Jobs
WHERE Employees.Age > 50 AND Jobs.[Hours
Taken] < 10
ORDER BY [Hours Taken] DESC;
```

- INSERT INTO is used to add new data to a table:

```
INSERT INTO Employees
VALUES ('1038849','David','Stott','32');
```

- UPDATE allows data currently stored in the database to be altered:

```
UPDATE Jobs
SET [Hours Taken] = 23
WHERE JobID = 14;
```

- DELETE deletes a row (record) from a database table:

```
DELETE FROM Employees
WHERE Forename = 'Matthew' AND Surname =
'Reid';
```

In addition to querying and modifying existing databases, commands such as CREATE DATABASE, CREATE TABLE and ALTER TABLE can be used to build a new database using only code.

Note that at Higher you are expected to know how SQL code works. It is unlikely that you will be asked to write SQL statements in an exam.

When data in a database is used as part of a calculation, the results are obtained and presented using queries and reports. A database should not store calculated data permanently in a table as this would result in a larger database file, which could slow response times to future queries.

A **report** is a formatted document used to display the results of a query. The document will contain the database fields being displayed, along with additional text, labels and graphics used to present the information in a user-friendly way. Generating a report may involve performing a query first and then opening the report to display the results, or the query may be embedded into the report itself thereby allowing both actions to be performed simultaneously. Reports may also include the results of calculations across multiple fields, for example, the total cost of multiple orders. These 'sums' are often displayed in the report's footer section.

What you should know

In your revision of this chapter, ensure that you are able to:

- ★ explain attributes, entities and relationships in an entity relationship diagram
- ★ create or modify an entity relationship diagram using a description of the data to be stored
- ★ explain the need to refine a design (normalisation) to reduce redundancy in a relational database
- ★ explain the purpose of a data dictionary
- ★ describe a query (fields, tables and search criteria) from a description of the data that is to be found
- ★ describe how scripts (such as SQL and PHP) may be used to extract, amend, insert and delete data in a database
- ★ explain how calculations are handled by relational databases
- ★ explain the purpose of a report and how a report is generated.

Questions ?

1 Explain why the cardinality of the relationship below is many-to-many. (1)

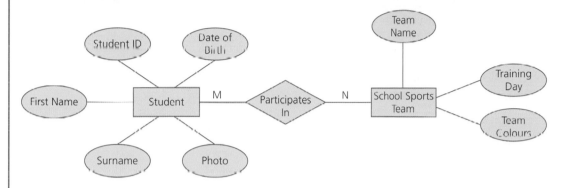

2 Explain why the failure to eliminate redundancy in a database design may cause problems later on when data in the implemented database is updated. (1)

3 A database is required to store information on the patients in a hospital and the staff who work there. Create an entity relationship diagram (showing only the entities and relationships) using the following information. (3)

The hospital has multiple wards, each of which is staffed by several nurses. Patients stay in a single ward, where they are assigned a single doctor. Doctors work in only one hospital but can be assigned many patients from a variety of wards. Nurses work in only one ward, and they look after all the patients in that ward.

4 Derek has just opened a shop that sells comic books. You have offered to design a database to catalogue his comic books, and you advise him to write down as much information about them as he can. Use the information he created below to create a first draft of an ER Diagram. Include entities, attributes, relationships and cardinality. (5)

Comics are uniquely identified by the name of the comic book and its issue number. Each comic is published by a publisher who employs authors to write comic books. Sometimes authors collaborate to write a comic. The stories in comic books are based around characters with superpowers. The characters, who are created by a single author, often appear in more than one comic. The most famous comic book authors have created many different characters.

The remaining questions are based on the following relational database, with three tables.

5 Newspapers

PaperID	PaperName	Circulation	ProducedIn
001	The Scotsman	29463	Edinburgh
002	The Daily Record	227639	Glasgow
003	Evening Express	47849	Aberdeen

Editors

EditorID	EditorName	DateStarted	PaperID
NA447843F	Ian Stewart	12/04/2009	001
LK234900S	Ewan Cameron	23/10/2012	003
HG872945K	Murray Foote	03/07/2014	002

Reporters

ReporterID	FirstName	Surname	Genre	PaperID
0129	Helen	Hunter	Sports	002
0029	Tracy	Tall	Middle East Affairs	002
1074	Iqbal	Azid	Politics	003
0273	Brian	McGill	NHS	001

Write an SQL query that will produce a list of the names of every reporter, ordered alphabetically by surname. (3)

6 A new sports reporter (ID 0348) called David Presley is starting work at the *Evening Express*. Write an SQL command to add his details to the database. (2)

7 *The Daily Record* has just moved its offices to Paisley. Write an SQL command to update the appropriate record. (3)

8 State the relationship that exists between the Newspapers table and the Reporters table. (1)

9 Describe how database software could be used to produce the output shown below. (3)

Newspaper Reporter List: The Daily Record		
FirstName	**Surname**	**Genre**
Helen	Hunter	Sports
Tracy	Tall	Middle East Affairs

## Chapter 13

Website design and implementation

Wire framing

Wire framing is an extremely important phase of web development. A **wire frame** is a skeleton outline of a website's layout or design. It contains no actual content but shows clearly the size and position of the main site components, such as navigation, text boxes, graphics and advertising.

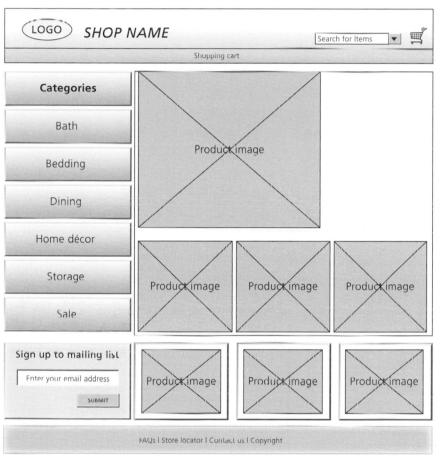

Figure 13.1 Wire framing

The advantages of wire framing are:
- Clients get a clear idea of the look and feel of the designed website without the need to create a full example of a working web page.
- Subsequent design changes are carried out efficiently as wire frames are fast to produce.
- The navigation structure of the website can be tested and refined before it is implemented.
- The usability and user interface of the website can be refined before implementation.
- The effectiveness of the layout can be evaluated before implementation.
- The development needs (including coding requirements) can be identified before the project begins.

Wire frames may be hand drawn on paper or produced in grayscale using specialised software such as Axure, Flairbuilder, Mockingbird and Omnigraffle. Some wire framing applications offer the facility to export the design as HTML, producing a template that can then be used by the developers to code the site content.

Normally a wire frame lacks any information on styles and colour as its purpose is to show functionality and behaviour. A **high definition wire frame** will include additional details such as font sizes, fonts and colour. A high definition wire frame takes longer to produce but closely resembles the final web page.

Site structures

When designing the content of a website the developers will create a map showing the structure of the site, including a brief note on the content of each page. The map will show the different levels in the site structure along with any links to external sites.

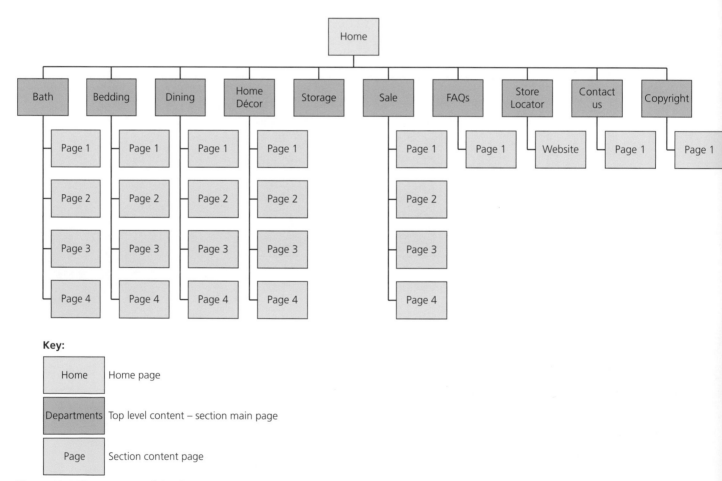

Figure 13.2 The structure of the site

HTML: page structures and meta tags

Web pages are coded using hypertext modelling language (HTML). HTML is a descriptive language used to describe the position and attributes of each object in the web page. HTML files contain only text, which may include the location of other stored files such as graphics, sound and video. These will then be loaded by the browser when the page is displayed.

The basic structure of an HTML document is shown below.

```
<html>
  <head>
  </head>
  <body>
  </body>
</html>
```

A pair of <html> </html> tags encloses the complete code. This tells the browser that the code contained between the tags is HTML. The content of the web page, visible to the user, is contained within the <body> </body> tags. The <head> </head> tags enclose all the head elements, such as a title, scripts, styles and meta information.

```
<head>
  <title>My Website</title>
  <meta name = "author" content="Greg Reid">
  <meta name = "description" content="test website
for HtP Computing">
  <meta name = "keywords" content="Higher,
Computing, Hodder, Pass">
  <meta http-equiv = "refresh" content="30">
</head>
```

The above example shows that the <meta> tag may have several properties, noting the author of the web page, a description of the page and a list of keywords associated with the page contents. The keywords are used by search engines to locate websites and pages that match search criteria entered by the user. The keywords are added to the search engine's database of websites.

The head elements are not displayed on the web page.

Cascading style sheets

As the world wide web evolved, developers realised that coding the required styles, alignments, margins, colours and positioning for each object, on each web page in a large site, was extremely time consuming.

The solution to this problem was to remove all the style information from the HTML and store it in a separate linked file, a cascading style sheet (CSS). This way, when the web page is displayed the styles are taken from the linked CSS file and applied to the tags in the HTML.

Cascading style sheet

HTML code

```
h1 {
    color:black;
    text-align:left;
    font-size:22px;
    }

p {
    font-family:helvetica;
    font-size:12px;
    word-spacing:2px;
    text-align:left;
    margin-left:20px;
    margin-right:20px;
    }
```

```
<html>

<head>
<title>Standard Algorithms</title>
<link rel="stylesheet" href="Standard Algorithms Style Sheet.css">
</head>

<body>
<h1>Standard Algorithms</h1>

<p>In programming there are a variety of algorithms that
programmers make use of over and over again.  These are called
Standard Algorithms.</p>
<p>Higher Computing requires that you are familiar with 5
standard algorithms.
</body>
</html>
```

Figure 13.3 A cascading style sheet

The advantage of style sheets is that they can be linked to multiple web pages, thus allowing a whole website to be controlled by the styles stored in a single file. If multiple CSS files are created then the same HTML document can be displayed in multiple views. This means that the page can be displayed on a small smartphone screen, for example, or read by a visually impaired user who prefers larger text. Additional code senses the device the web page is being viewed on and loads the appropriate CSS file.

IDs and classes are user-defined styles that are not associated with a specific HTML tag. While IDs can only be assigned to a single tag, classes may be used multiple times.

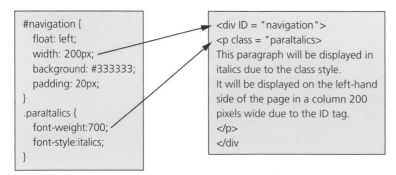

Figure 13.4 Cascading style sheet showing an ID and a class

If two styles are applied to the same object the browser uses the following rule to decide which to apply: 'IDs are of most importance, then classes, then HTML tag styles.'

Appendices of CSS and HTML code are located at the back of this book (pages 82 and 84).

Interactive and dynamic web pages

When a user enjoys using a website and perceives the website as being useful they are more likely to keep returning to it. For commercial websites in particular this may be the most important consideration when designing the website. One way to improve users' experience is to create an interactive, dynamic website.

Interaction offers the user options to click on. The website may respond to these clicks by:
- changing the content of the page
- playing a video or animation
- moving an object
- revealing an object
- giving feedback to the user.

A web page that changes its contents with or without interaction by the user is a **dynamic** web page. One of the most common uses of dynamic content is to have an area of the page that displays a repeating set of graphics.

To create interactive and dynamic content requires the use of one or more of the following technologies.
- HTML and CSS – to create dynamic layouts that react to different hardware or user selections.
- JavaScript – to animate page contents, allow user keyboard input and response, load new page data or submit data to a server.
- PHP – to link to SQL databases, collect information from users and dynamically generate web pages using database data.
- Flash – to create full multimedia content, such as games or slide shows.

Database-driven websites

Any dynamic website that allows its users to search through stored information is using web/database technology. The diagram below represents the connection between the technologies involved.

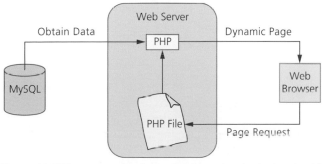

Figure 13.5 The connection between the technologies involved in dynamic websites

For example, the following steps may be carried out if an Amazon user searches for 'mountain bikes valued between £200 and £400'.

1 The web page will use embedded program code to send the search criteria to Amazon's web server.
2 A script on the web server will then be run, requesting that the correct information be filtered from database fields and records stored on a database server.
3 The database server will return the requested information on mountain bikes worth >£200 and <£400 to the web server.
4 Program code on the web server will then generate an HTML document that includes the information received from the database server.
5 The HTML document is then received and displayed by the user's browser.

Note that the dynamic web page created in this process exists solely for that user.

The most common scripting language used to dynamically generate web pages using database data is PHP. Other languages, such as JSP, ASP, PERL and Cold Fusion, compete with PHP for dominance.

What you should know

In your revision of this chapter, ensure that you are able to:
★ explain the purpose of the design methodology known as wire framing
★ explain the advantages of wire framing for web developers and their clients
★ describe the use of site structure diagrams in design
★ explain the basic structure of an HTML document
★ explain the use of meta tags
★ state the advantages of using cascading style sheets to control the layout and look of a web page
★ write and explain the purpose of simple tag styles, IDs and classes
★ explain the terms 'interactivity' and 'dynamic' in reference to web pages
★ describe how interactive, dynamic web pages are created
★ describe how web pages are dynamically generated using information from databases.

Questions ?

1 Gillian has created a website about her pet dog, a Labradoodle called Penny. On the website she discusses feeding routines, local walks that she takes Penny on, as well as how to brush and cut Penny's long coat. The website refreshes only when the user manually clicks Refresh in their browser. Write three meta tags suitable for Gillian's website. (3)

2 A client has asked to see a full colour design of their website. State the design methodology that should be used. (1)

3 State the HTML tag that contains the visual content of a website. (1)

4 Look carefully at the sections of a HTML and linked CSS file shown below.

Will the 'ID introStyle' or 'p tag' style be applied to the text? Explain your answer. (2)

Cascading style sheet

```
p {
    font-family:helvetica;
    font-size:12px;
    text-align:left;
    }

#introStyle{
    font-family:times new roman;
    font-size:16px;
    text-align:center;
    }
```

HTML code

```
<html>

<head>
<title>Standard Algorithms</title>
<link rel="stylesheet" href="Style Sheet.css">
</head>

<body>
<div ID = "introStyle">
<p>Computing Science Higher</p>
</div>
</body>

</html>
```

5 A visually impaired user clicks a button on a website. This causes the page layout to change to a simplified version with enlarged text, improving the usability of the page for the user. Describe the technologies that could be used to implement the above. (2)

6 The home page of a clothing website contains an area that advertises the site's ten most popular items. The items are displayed repeatedly, one after the other, for two seconds each. If the user clicks on an item they are taken to the page for that item of clothing.
Explain why this is an example of a database-driven, interactive, dynamic website. (3)

7 State why the process of generating a web page on a database-driven website is often called server-side scripting. (1)

## Chapter 14

User interfaces and types of user

Usability

The usability of an information system should take account of the following factors:

- Navigation – navigation should be consistent (same colour and positions on each page/screen) and not too cluttered. Multi-level collapsible menus can be used to reduce the number of options visible on the page.
- Screen layout – layouts should be consistent, with similar objects grouped and always positioned in the same place. If a screen is too cluttered the designer should consider creating two simpler pages instead.
- Input style – drop-down menus, list boxes and radio buttons can simplify forms, reducing errors.
- Disabilities – colour schemes should be selected to account for colour blindness, alternate text on graphics may inform sight-impaired users about the images' contents, alternate CSS can change the layout and text sizes to suit a variety of disabilities.

Target users

Matching the user interface to the intended audience of an information system will ensure the greatest possibility of attracting users. The amount of text, reading age level of text, use of technical language, buttons, sound and animation should all be considered by the developers when designing the user interface. Pitching the interface to the wrong user profile may seriously affect the usability of the information system.

What you should know

In your revision of this chapter, ensure that you are able to:
- ★ discuss important aspects of user interface design
- ★ identify methods used to match a user interface to a selected audience.

Questions

1 Examine the figure below and suggest three ways to improve the design of the user interface. (1)

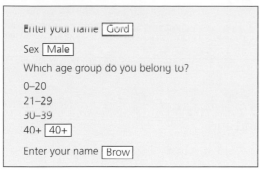

2 Including videos on a training website may exclude hearing-impaired users from accessing all the content on the site. Describe a solution that would allow videos to be viewed without excluding this group. (1)

## Chapter 15

Compressing media types

Information systems such as websites, multimedia applications and databases will include one or more of the following data types:

- text
- graphics
- sound
- video.

The large file sizes of some of these data types (particularly sound and video) are associated with the following problems:

- Longer download/opening times.
- Increased storage requirements.
- More demanding hardware requirements.

The solution to large files is to reduce the amount of data stored in the file by use of compression techniques. File compression techniques can be categorised into two types:

Lossy compression	Once the file is compressed the original data file can never be recreated (uncompressed). The data removed by lossy compression is lost forever.
Lossless compression	Lossless file compression techniques encode the data in a way that the file may be uncompressed, recreating the original file.

Graphic compression techniques

Run length encoding

The RLE compression algorithm analyses a bit-mapped image for repeating pixel colours. Where a colour appears more than once in a row, a single value for that colour is stored, along with a note of the number of times the colour is repeated.

Before

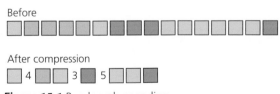

After compression

Figure 15.1 Run length encoding

Run length encoding is a lossless technique.

LZW encoding

LZW encoding compression algorithms look for repeating patterns of pixels. A dictionary of these patterns is created as each repeating set of pixels is identified. The dictionary is used to replace the repeating patterns with a code. The new data and the dictionary are both saved in the compressed file.

LZW encoding is also a lossless technique, as files are easily uncompressed using the stored data and dictionary. Graphic interchange format (gif) files are compressed using the LZW algorithm.

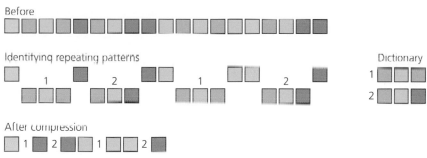

Figure 15.2 LZW encoding

DCT encoding

Discrete cosine transform encoding applies a mathematical algorithm (based on a cosine wave) to groups of 64 (8x8) pixels. Each group of 64 pixels is saved in a compressed form. When the graphic is viewed, each group is uncompressed to recreate an approximation of the original group. The groups of pixels are joined to create the complete image.

DCT encoding is used in the jpeg (jpg) standard file format and is a lossy technique.

Vector graphic encoding

A vector graphic stores the properties of objects using text. Due to the nature of the file (lots of similar objects are often being stored) there may be repeating patterns of characters in the text file. Using a similar technique to LZW encoding, these patterns may be stored in a shorter form and kept in a dictionary.

An svg (scalable vector graphic) file may be compressed in this way.

Sound compression techniques

Perceptual noise shaping

MPEG1 Layer 3 (mp3) files use a variety of techniques known as perceptual noise shaping to compress a sound to approximately a tenth of the original file size. Despite this 90 per cent compression, an mp3 file retains remarkable sound quality because each of the techniques listed below focuses on removing data that the human ear can't easily hear.

- When a quiet sound exists next to a loud sound of a similar frequency, the quiet sound is removed.

- Very low and very high frequency sounds are removed, as the human ear finds it difficult to hear these.
- Low base sounds are changed from stereo to a single mono sound as the human ear cannot detect the direction from which base sounds are coming.
- If the difference can't be detected, some sounds are encoded using lower quality settings.

Video compression techniques

Inter frame compression

This type of compression stores only the information that has changed between each frame of a video. A complete reference frame called an I-frame is stored at regular intervals (approximately every twenty frames). The compression algorithm searches for blocks of pixels that don't change between each of the frames that follow the I-frame. Rather than storing these complete blocks of pixels again, the algorithm stores the position of the blocks in the I-frame. The amount of compression achieved will be determined by how many differences there are between each of the frames.

Figure 15.3 Inter frame compression

Intra frame compression

Intra frame compression treats each frame of the video as a separate bit-mapped graphic and compresses the frames using similar techniques to those discussed earlier.

Codecs

Both inter and intra frame compression techniques may be applied to the frames in a video file; the accompanying sound for the video would also be compressed. The variety of techniques used for a video's images and sound are stored in a 'codec'. In order to watch the compressed video, the video-playing software must have the same codec installed.

What you should know

Questions like 'Why are files compressed?' would more likely be National 5 level than Higher. When revising this topic, focus on being able to **apply** the knowledge. Think about, for example:

★ which types of compression are suited to particular scenarios
★ how compression is achieved in the different file types discussed
★ how the data in the file affects the success of a compression algorithm.

Questions

These questions are all based around applying the knowledge in this topic.

1 Explain why it is important that video files displayed by a browser are compressed. (1)
2 Explain why both RLE and LZW compression algorithms are unsuitable to compress a bit-mapped photograph of a landscape stored using 24-bit colour depth. (2)
3 Which type of compression would be most suitable to compress the following graphic? (2)

The
Media
Society

4 From the description of vector graphic compression, is the algorithm used a lossless or lossy compression technique? Explain your answer. (2)
5 Explain why the amount of inter frame compression achieved would be minimal in a high action movie with lots of fast movement. (2)

Coding in databases and web pages

Please refer to Chapters 12 and 13 for more information on how coding is used to create, manipulate and enhance databases and web pages.

Client-side scripting

Client-side scripting refers to program code that is embedded in documents (usually HTML documents) that are viewed on the user's computer. The programs (or scripts) will be run by the user's browser or similar software. The most common language used in client-side scripting is JavaScript. The figure below shows how a JavaScript function can be embedded in the <head> tag of an HTML document. The function is called when a button is clicked in the <body> of the document.

```
<html>
<head>

<script>
function changeText() {
    document.getElementById("changeThis").innerHTML = "Change text to this.";
}
</script>

</head>

<body>
<h1>JavaScript Example</h1>
<p id="changeThis">Start with this text.</p>
<button type="button" onclick="changeText()">Click Me</button>
</body>

</html>
```

Figure 16.1 HTML and embedded JavaScript function

Client-side scripting is often used to ensure that valid data has been entered into forms. This ensures that only complete, valid data is sent to servers to be processed.

Server-side scripting

Server-side scripting refers to program code that is executed by the server. PHP and ASP are server-side scripting languages that may be used to:

- validate web forms
- generate new web pages by dynamically creating an HTML document that is returned to the user's browser for display
- create, edit and query databases (when used with SQL).

The example below shows an HTML form that activates the 'welcome.php' file when the Submit button on the form is clicked.

```html
<html>
<body>

<form action="welcome.php" method="post">
Name: <input type="text" name="name"><br>
E-mail: <input type="text" name="email"><br>
<input type="submit">
</form>

</body>
</html>
```

Figure 16.2 HTML form with server-side scripting

Client-side vs server-side

Any programs or data that are executed or stored on a client's computer are easily accessed. This makes them less secure and prone to hacking. Programs and data stored on the server may be protected by a firewall and are therefore difficult to access. Data validation, such as checking a username and password, should therefore always be carried out using server-side scripting.

If a program is executed on the client's computer it reduces the processing load on the server. This reduction may be quite significant on a busy website.

Client-side scripting may also reduce the number of times that data is passed from the client's computer to the server, reducing data traffic.

Some programs/scripts may require additional browser plugins (for example Flash and Java) to run. Developers would have to take this into account, as the need for plugins may potentially reduce the number of users of a website. If programs are implemented server-side the developers have to install additional technologies only on their own hardware.

Optimisation

Research has shown that users will wait for a very short time for a page to load. If it takes too long they will look elsewhere. A website can be coded in ways that optimise load times. For example:

- Storing scripts and styles externally reduces the file size of the page.
- Placing JavaScript at the end of HTML documents allows the visible part of the page to load first.
- Making use of browser caching reduces the need to download CSS, scripts and images multiple times.
- Removing unnecessary HTML and CSS styles reduces the size of the files being downloaded and displayed.
- Placing style sheets at the top of the document, thereby ensuring that content can begin to load immediately rather than being cached until the required styles can be accessed.

To improve the likelihood that a search will find a web page, developers can optimise their website. Search engines use databases to store information on keywords and the popularity of a website. Improved use of keywords in meta tags and increasing the number of internal links within the website can improve its chances of appearing higher up in search results.

Beta testing

When an information system has been tested internally and any errors fixed, it will be released as a beta version. The system will be tested by persons not associated with the developers. These people may be volunteers. For more information on testing, refer to Chapter 5.

Compatibility issues

To execute without errors all software must be compatible with the system on which it is running.

Hardware factors to be considered include available RAM, storage requirements and processing capability. If software is developed to be multi-platform (for example, desktop PC, tablet computer and smartphone) then factors such as peripheral devices should also be considered, as the input and output devices may differ.

Software factors include compatibility with operating systems (both current and older versions), viewing software (such as browsers or readers), and plugin requirements. Plugins are usually downloaded and installed within another application to improve its functionality. Many modern information system technologies are not platform-specific. HTML, JavaScript, Java, Flash, PHP and SQL were all designed to run on any system and may require only the occasional plugin update.

What you should know

In your revision of this chapter, ensure that you are able to:

★ state a definition of client-side scripting
★ state a definition of server-side scripting
★ discuss the differences between the above, including the advantages and disadvantages of each
★ explain common techniques used to optimise download speeds of web pages
★ state a definition of beta testing, including where it takes place and who is involved
★ state the factors that should be considered to ensure an information system is compatible with the computer system on which it is running.

Questions

1 A student creates a quiz web page with ten questions and ten input boxes for the user's answers. She writes a JavaScript program to check the user's answers and embeds the script in the HTML source code of the web page.
   a) Explain whether this is an example of client- or server-side scripting. (2)
   b) Explain why this is a poor solution to the quiz web page she was trying to implement. (2)
2 State the technology used to prevent access to a server and that ensures that server-side scripting is more secure than client-side. (1)
3 Describe why CSS styles should be stored in an external file and why the link to the file should be located near the top of an HTML document's code. (2)
4 Web authoring applications contain pre-made templates with styles. A developer uses a template but uses only four of the 20 in-built styles in their web page. Explain the possible effect of this on the load time of the page and discuss how the page could be optimised. (2)
5 David clicks on a link to a website containing 200 Flash games. Some of the games work fine for him, while others display an error when he tries to play them. Explain why David can play only some of the games and suggest a solution to his problem. (2)

## Chapter 17

Technical implementation

When designing, implementing and using an information system, users must consider the system requirements.

Hardware requirements

A variety of **input devices** may be required to create an information system. These may be digital cameras, digital video cameras and/or scanners that are used to capture graphics and video. A keyboard, touchscreen or microphone with voice recognition software may be used to enter text. A microphone or midi keyboard may be used to capture sound. Some information systems input data using specialist input devices such as barcode scanners, QR readers or mark sense card readers (where choices are made using small marks on paper that are then read by a scanner, e.g. as used for lottery tickets).

Figure 17.1 Barcode and QR code

Information systems are created to be viewed or printed. While early information systems had to consider only desktop screens (with their varied resolutions and colour depths), modern systems are often designed for screens ranging from a small smartphone to a large LCD desktop monitor. Many of these devices also have the capability to rotate screen images from landscape to portrait. Information systems will use technologies such as CSS to build software capable of sensing and reacting to different screen sizes, resolutions and rotations.

Developers of software, such as information systems, must take account of the processing power required to run their software. The processing capability of a computer system is determined by factors such as the type of processor (bus widths and number of cores), cache memory and the clock speed of the processor. If the software requires more processing power than is available it will run slowly and be less responsive than intended.

Another consideration is the amount of available memory on a computer system. This is more of a concern with smaller devices, such as smart phones, where RAM is likely to be limited.

Software requirements

Software can run only if it is compatible with the operating system of the computer on which it is running. If an information system is created as an executable program it will probably be produced for a specific operating system. If the information system is produced as documents to be displayed by applications software (for example, HTML documents displayed by a browser), then compatibility with the operating system may be assumed.

Software that runs on multiple platforms (different operating systems and hardware) is described as **portable**. The more portable the software is, the larger the potential numbers of users. The use of non-platform-specific technologies such as HTML, PHP and SQL improves the potential portability of information systems.

Figure 17.2 Examples of operating systems

An information system may be distributed as **licensed software**, where users are required to purchase single or multiple licences to legally use the information system. Software may also be distributed for free as **shareware**, which is often limited to 30 days' use or requires the user to make a small payment to unlock all the features of the software. If the information system is entirely free it may be distributed as **freeware**. Freeware software will usually be licensed simply to prevent users from modifying the software. It may also be the case that users only pay for the data in an information system.

During the creation of an information system a variety of applications may be used to create and edit files. Applications may be proprietary or open source. **Proprietary** software is commercially produced, meaning it will be fully supported by phone helplines and website forums. Proprietary software should be error-free but will have functions limited to those it had when it was purchased. **Open source** software is created and maintained by a community of users and programmers. Anybody with the required skill set can modify, improve and republish open source software. This means the software is constantly evolving, although not necessarily in a way that suits all its users. Support may vary as it depends on the willingness of the community to help resolve issues. Note that open source software will be more prone to tampering – such as virus/ Trojan insertion – as the source code may be edited by anyone.

Storage requirements

Information systems may require internal, external and online (cloud) storage to distribute software, install software, store data used by or created by the software, and create backups of data.

Data storage is the most important aspect of any information system. Web pages, database data and applications will usually be stored on an internal hard disk drive. Hard disk drives are large capacity (>1TB) magnetic storage devices that offer the fast access speeds required to deliver the loading times required by web pages and database updates/ queries. Data may also be stored on external devices such as solid state USB Flash drives (devices that store data on to Flash memory) or on external hard disk drives. The speed of data transfer to and from these devices will be limited by the type of interface used to connect them. The two most common interface types are Universal Serial Bus (USB) and Firewire.

Software may be distributed on optical disks, like CDs, DVDs or Blu-rays. Such disks are normally read-only ROM versions, which prevent accidental deletion or modification of the distributed software. Data stores such as databases will be copied from read-only distribution media to allow editing when tables, records or fields are added or deleted. In some circumstances distribution media may need to be rewritable (CD-RW, DVD-RW, Blu-ray-RW), allowing data to be updated without copying to another storage medium. Web-based information systems require no distribution.

The majority of executable programs will be installed on to the backing storage of a computer system before use. The amount of backing storage required by software should be carefully considered as part of its design, as excessive requirements could cause installation problems for users with limited available storage.

Information systems' data must be backed up to ensure against accidental or malicious data loss. A **backup strategy** should be considered when systems are designed and implemented. Backups should be taken regularly and be kept in a secure, remote location to ensure they are not also vulnerable to any factor that caused initial data loss. Setups like RAID (redundant array of independent disks) may be installed to protect against hardware failure. RAID uses banks of hard disk drives to produce two copies of every file on separate disks. If one hard disk in the bank fails, the missing files can be recreated on a new drive from the duplicate copies on the other hard disks in the array.

Networking/connectivity requirements

Many information systems are 'multi-user' systems as they are accessed simultaneously by multiple users. The data being accessed is stored centrally on a file server, database server or web server. It is becoming increasingly common for companies to rent remote server storage space, known as **cloud** storage, rather than paying for and maintaining their own servers. There are three types of cloud storage:

- Public – the files stored can be seen by anyone with the capability to connect to the server.
- Private – the files are accessible only by a select group of individuals, for example the employees of a company.
- Hybrid – some of the data on the server is publicly available and some is private.

Nearly all websites use cloud storage. Site owners pay a subscription to a web-hosting company to provide storage for their site content and internet connectivity to allow users to access the site.

Cloud computing may also be used to deliver services other than storage. Applications installed remotely may be downloaded to a user's computer system when needed. The user never purchases these applications but instead pays a set monthly user fee, or may pay for the time they use each application. This may have financial advantages for companies as they do not have to pay IT staff to install, maintain or update applications, nor do they have to pay for the latest versions of software as these are often updated automatically by the provider. Other services include network telephone systems, video conferencing, email and virtual servers.

Cloud computing has the advantage of being quickly scalable. A company that requires greater storage or improved services simply changes the terms of their contract to have immediate access to the extra facilities they need. The rise of cloud computing can be directly attributed to increases in bandwidths offered by telecommunications companies. As bandwidths continue to increase it is likely that cloud services will also expand and develop.

What you should know

In your revision of this chapter, ensure that you are able to:

★ discuss the hardware required to design, implement and use an information system
★ discuss the software required to design, implement and use an information system
★ discuss the storage required to design, implement and use an information system
★ explain the uses of a variety of hardware devices in storing data
★ discuss the requirement to back up data and the strategies involved
★ discuss cloud storage features and facilities
★ explain the term 'web hosting'.

Questions

1 Explain why hardware backup solutions like RAID are not effective against hacking threats. (2)

2 Smartphone manufacturers provide regular updates to their phones' operating systems. Explain why older phones often reach a point where they can no longer install new updates. (1)

3 State one advantage of producing an information system capable of running on multiple platforms. (1)

4 Smartphones have limited storage capabilities in comparison to a desktop computer system. Describe a solution that would allow smartphone users to access more files than their phone is capable of storing. (1)

5 A software company shares production tasks between programmers based in several different offices. Software is regularly shared with clients during production by allowing them to access prototypes of the software. Explain the type of cloud storage in this scenario. (2)

## Chapter 18

Security risks and precautions

Since the early 1990s the internet and world wide web have grown from being used exclusively by governments, businesses, researchers and computer enthusiasts to being part of everyday life for most people. In line with this growth has been the rise of online security threats – and an entire industry built around preventing them.

Security risks

Capturing the personal details of internet users allows criminals to commit a variety of illegal acts.

If enough information can be learned about a user, criminals can use the stolen information to apply for credit cards, set up bank accounts, access free medical care or even apply for a passport. This is known as **identity theft**. If a user's bank details are stolen, **online fraud** can be committed. This could take the form of illegally purchasing goods or transferring money to the thief's bank account.

Some common methods used to capture personal details are:
- Spyware – small programs that secretly record the browsing habits of a user. Captured information may be sold to companies who will target that user's interests.
- Phishing – emails or websites that trick users into entering personal details, which are then used illegally

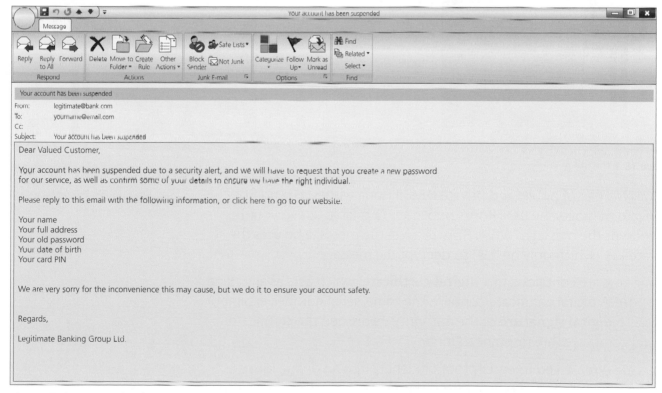

Figure 18.1 An example of a phishing email

- Keylogging – programs that secretly record every keyboard key pressed and save them to a file. The usernames and passwords contained in the file are then used by hackers to access a variety of online websites (e.g. bank accounts, shopping, auction, social media).

Any company, organisation or individual who runs an online business must ensure that precautions are in place to prevent security risks such as DOS attacks. A **denial of service (DOS) attack** is designed to prevent a user from accessing a computer system, server or website. Although a variety of methods is used in DOS attacks, most have the same purpose: to create a situation where the resources of the attacked system are flooded with so many processing requests that the system can no longer carry out its intended purpose.

Security precautions

One of the oldest methods used to hide data from unauthorised individuals is **encryption**. Pairs of encryption keys – public and private – are used to scramble data so effectively that it cannot be read by anyone who intercepts it.

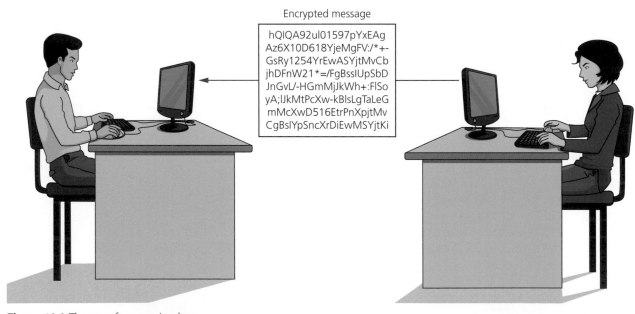

Encrypted message

hQIQA92ul01597pYxEAg
Az6X10D618YjeMgFV:/*+-
GsRy1254YrEwASYjtMvCb
jhDFnW21*=/FgBssIUpSbD
JnGvL/-HGmMjJkWh+:FlSo
yA;lJkMtPcXw-kBlsLgTaLeG
mMcXwD516EtrPnXpjtMv
CgBslYpSncXrDiEwMSYjtKi

Figure 18.2 The use of encryption keys

Rory has a pair of public and private keys. If Fiona wishes to send Rory a private message, she uses Rory's public key (available to everyone) to encrypt the message. When Rory receives the message he uses the private key (which only he has) to decrypt the message.

Public keys are contained in a **digital certificate**, which acts as an online passport. A digital certificate contains the name, serial number, expiration date and **digital signature** of the authority that issued the certificate. Digital certificates are resistant to forgery.

Users are often asked to enter proof of identity into an online form. Server-side validation of online forms improves security (please refer to Chapter 16 for more information on server-side scripting).

Human attributes such as fingerprints and retina patterns may be used instead of passwords to gain access to systems and data. These systems work by taking measurements of these unique patterns, called **biometrics**. Biometric data is significantly harder to forge than conventional passwords.

What you should know

In your revision of this chapter, ensure that you are able to:

★ describe a variety of security threats to users' personal information
★ describe how personal data may be misused by criminals
★ explain the effect that a DOS attack has on a computer system
★ explain how data can be transmitted securely using public and private encryption keys
★ state definitions of the terms 'digital certificate' and 'digital signature'
★ explain the term 'biometrics'
★ describe how the use of biometrics improves security.

Questions

1 Bethany receives an email offering her discounts on clothing she recently browsed on a well-known shopping website. State the type of software that Bethany may have on her computer system without her knowledge. (1)
2 A hacker writes a small program designed to request data from a web server 100,000 times a second. State the security risk the website owner has failed to prevent occurring. (1)
3 Explain why public and private key encryption works only with pairs of keys. (1)
4 Explain how you could ensure that a public encryption key is authentic. (1)
5 Explain why fingerprint recognition makes newer smartphones more secure than older technologies. (2)

## Chapter 19

Legal implications

The following Acts of Parliament apply to the use of computer hardware, software and communications media.

Computer Misuse Act

The Computer Misuse Act makes it illegal to perform the following actions with a computer system:

- **'Unauthorised access to computer material.'** This means the act of using software and hardware to access data unlawfully without permission (hacking). Hackers may go on to delete, steal or alter data, but the crime has been committed as soon as the data is accessed.
- **'Unauthorised access with intent to commit or facilitate commission of further offences.'** Hackers may also be charged if they intend to commit further crimes with the data they steal (for example fraud, bribery, selling the data).
- **'Unauthorised acts with intent to impair the operation of computer systems.'** Examples of this may include using a DOS attack to crash a website or deliberately spreading computer viruses. It is interesting to note that creating a virus is itself not illegal, only the deliberate spreading of one.

Copyright Designs and Patents Act

The Copyright Designs and Patents Act covers the illegal broadcasting, performing, copying, adapting, issuing, renting or lending of someone's work. The 'work' may include:

- Literature – novels, short stories, poetry, articles, research documents, tutorials, etc.
- Artwork – traditional art or computer-created graphics.
- Films – full length movies to short animations.
- Music – songs, albums, ringtones.

Only the creator of the work or the licensee (the publisher) may instigate court proceedings following copyright infringement. If an employee creates as part of their job any of the above works, their employer owns the rights to the work.

Examples of infringements include: copying CDs, downloading films from peer-to-peer networks, installing software without the purchase of a licence, or copied graphics from a website.

Communications Act

The Communications Act deals with the deliberate abuse of telecommunications media, including phone lines, Wi-Fi points, mobile networks, television, broadcasting and postal services. The following are illegal under the act:

- **'Dishonestly obtaining electronic communication services.'** This may include cloning a mobile phone SIM so that the original owner gets charged for your calls, or using a Wi-Fi connection without the owner's permission.
- **'Possession of equipment used to dishonestly obtain communications services.'** This could include the use of software/hardware to access a protected network, take control of a radio frequency, block a television signal or produce clones of satellite TV cards.
- **'Improper use of a public electronic communications network.'** This section of the Act is broken by users of email, social networks, forums or mobile phones who send messages of an offensive, obscene or threatening nature.

Regulation of Investigatory Powers Act

The Regulation of Investigatory Powers Act (RIPA) was created to give government, police and security services the powers to intercept communications or monitor internet use in order to prevent or detect criminal activity.

The Act is enforced through surveillance techniques and undercover agents or by forcing the owners of encrypted information to provide the passwords required to decrypt the data. Under this Act internet service providers (ISPs) are also required to co-operate with requests to monitor suspects' internet habits.

RIPA has been criticised by human rights groups, who claim that the Act infringes people's rights to privacy. The Government states that the surveillance and monitoring powers of the Act require the personal approval of the Home Secretary and are used only when serious crime or a threat to national security is suspected.

What you should know

In your revision of this chapter, ensure that you:

- ★ memorise the exact title of each Act, as a missing or incorrect word may lose you marks in an exam
- ★ understand the details of each Act to the point where you can consider and discuss the relevance of one or more of the Acts in a given scenario.

Questions ?

Explain the relevance of one or more of the Acts of Parliament to each of the following scenarios.

1 Samalia runs a social networking website that is used to discuss political issues of the day. To encourage debate, Samalia copies articles published by national newspapers and publishes them on the website. (2)

2 Derek is a keen computer games player. He downloads and uses software to illegally change the level of account he has within his favourite game. This has the effect of giving him access to additional facilities and features that would usually be purchased for £100. (2)

3 Ross has used the world wide web to research how data is stored on satellite TV account cards. He has used this information to build a machine capable of cloning the account cards. He plans to sell the cards for £30 each. (2)

4 Carolann lives above a café in the centre of town. Each day she uses the café's pay-per-hour Wi-Fi signal, without the café's knowledge, to organise her substantial DVD pirating empire. (6)

## Chapter 20

Economic, social and environmental impacts

Computer hardware, software and stored data now influence every aspect of society in a variety of positive and negative ways.

Economic influences

Computer systems and the programs and information systems that run on them allow us to process ever greater quantities of data faster. This allows companies to:

- manufacture more while spending less
- communicate faster, both within the company and with clients
- target potential customers more effectively through information gathering
- make more informed decisions regarding future products based on market analysis.

The **competitive advantage** gained through computerisation is such that many companies simply can't afford to stand still.

The growth of the world wide web has created a **global marketplace**. International sales were previously dominated by large companies. Now even the smallest home business with a presence on the world wide web may receive orders from any corner of the world.

The computerisation of any business can create significant **business costs**. Investments must be made in hardware, software production, installation, and training and hiring IT staff to maintain any new systems. Although significant, these costs should be recuperated through the growth and increased profits of the business.

Any initial investment in computerisation will have subsequent costs as systems require maintenance, replacement and upgrading. The **maintainability** of a new system should be properly considered through recruitment of suitably skilled staff and financial planning.

Any ambitious company aims for growth. The ability to adapt to changing hardware requirement (e.g. from a sudden increase in website hits) or software requirements (e.g. a sudden need for increased security measures) is called **scalability**. As previously mentioned, many companies now use cloud providers to supply the systems they require, as these providers often specialise in scaling up system capabilities very quickly. If a company maintains its own systems, its staff will have to be competent enough to perform the necessary tasks when required.

Social influences

The increase in social media, forums, chat rooms, online reviews, online news and online gaming have created **online communities** with millions of daily users. This has effectively removed borders and barriers, creating a **global community** of connected users that is unprecedented in our world's history. In addition, portable devices such as tablets and smartphones ensure that access to these communities is no longer limited to desktop computer access.

With increased, often anonymous, communication comes new debate regarding the following:

- Censorship and freedom of speech – where is the line drawn between an individual's right to comment and another individual's right not to be attacked? Across the world countries and governments have implemented legislation ranging from total control over what an individual views and posts to total freedom of the same.
- Privacy – does an individual have the right to remain totally anonymous at all times, even when they break the law?
- Encryption – does an individual have the right to hide the content of every message they send and every file they store, even if the contents are obscene or threaten national security?

Environmental factors

The use of a computer system creates a **carbon footprint** for the lifetime of the device, as significant quantities of electricity will be required during its use. Any production of electrical energy creates a carbon footprint. The software written for the computer system will similarly have taken thousands of hours of computer time and energy to produce.

The manufacture of a computer system also creates a carbon footprint as every component of a computer system must be manufactured, a process that requires energy and raw materials (including some rare metals).

The disposal of a computer system requires energy to transport the system to a waste site and to recycle the raw materials.

Computer systems may also be of benefit to the environment, as there are many examples of computers saving energy. Computer-manufactured products are produced more accurately and with less waste, which saves energy. Computer-controlled heating systems produce efficiency savings, thus reducing energy bills. Data analysis of delivery routes will discover the most efficient way of making deliveries to houses, again saving energy.

What you should know

In your revision of this chapter, ensure that you are able to:

★ describe the economic influence of computer systems and software
★ describe the initial investments required to implement a computerised system
★ discuss the influences (both positive and negative) of new technologies on society
★ understand the debates regarding social responsibility and monitoring
★ explain the term 'lifetime carbon footprint' of a computer system
★ describe some environmental benefits of computer system use.

Questions

1 A cloud service provider hosts a website for a client. As the client's website becomes more successful the web server automatically begins to share the task of processing user requests with a second web server. State of what this is a good example. (1)
2 Explain the term 'lifetime carbon footprint' in relation to a smartphone. (3)
3 A hotel website allows its customers to review their stay in the hotel. Discuss one economic implication and one social implication that the hotel should consider when allowing customers to write reviews. (2)
4 Describe three reasons why implementing a database-driven commercial website may increase sales. (3)

## Chapter 21

ISDD unit assessment preparation

Purpose of assessment

All Curriculum for Excellence (CfE) courses are created around **outcomes** and **standards**. Outcomes note what you must be taught in each unit, while the standards supply the details of how each outcome will be covered. The purpose of unit assessments is to gather evidence that each student has met the appropriate standards.

CfE unit assessments are graded as a pass or a fail. There are no marks. To pass the assessment you must pass all of the assessment standards listed below.

Outcomes	Assessment standards
1 Develop an information system using appropriate development tools.	Use design and development methodologies.
	Create a structure with complex links.
	Include a good user interface design.
	Write some code.
	Include different types of media.
	Find and correct errors.
	Test the linked structure using given criteria.
2 Consider the factors involved in the design and implementation of an information system.	Discuss functions (range and types of user).
	Discuss hardware and software requirements.
	Discuss storage and connectivity.
	Discuss security risks and precautions.
	Discuss legal and environmental implications.
	Discuss economic and social impacts.

Conditions of assessment

- Outcome 1 will be assessed through a practical task.
- Outcome 2 will be assessed through a written report.

All assessments will take place in class without assistance.

Assessments are 'open book', which means you can refer to any resources (workbooks, tutorials, textbooks, the world wide web) to help you carry out the practical tasks or write up your report.

There is no set time limit for each assessment, but as your teacher has a course to complete it would be unrealistic to assume that you will get as long as you want to complete the task and report.

Possible tasks

Outcome 1 could be assessed by asking you to create:
- a relational database with a few tables
- a multi-level website with internal and external hyperlinks, some coding (JavaScript) and a search facility

- a multimedia application with similar complexity to the website
- an expert system with similar complexity to the website.

For each of these you would be given a topic and relevant data to include in the information system. To meet the standards you will have to design, implement, correct errors in and test your product.

Outcome 2 will take the form of a report in which you will discuss each of the standards in relation to the information system you created in Outcome 1. For example, you may have to discuss the storage requirements of your database or the user interface of your multimedia application.

Preparation

If you ask your teacher what type of task you will be given (relational database, website, multimedia application or expert system), you will be able to practise using the software required to implement the information system.

Read your theory notes before the assessment, concentrating on the standards listed in Outcome 2. Improving your knowledge of these areas of the Higher course will make the task of writing your report easier.

Advice

The assessments are not designed to test your memory. Remember that this is an open book assessment. If you can't remember how to link two database tables or write some of the JavaScript code, look it up!

Complete each task. This may appear obvious, but many of the assessments that teachers hand back to students to redo have nothing wrong with them, they simply have parts missing. Read the instructions carefully to ensure you haven't missed anything.

Concentrate. If you are too relaxed at the beginning of the task, you will rush the end of it. Your report will lack detail and you may fail one or more standards.

What happens if I fail?

If you fail an outcome or standard you will not be asked to resit the whole assessment. Your teacher will offer you one opportunity to attempt part of the assessment again. Your teacher is allowed to advise you on which standards you have not met but is not allowed to tell you how to fix your mistakes.

If you continue to fail outcomes and standards you will not be allowed to sit the exam at the end of the year. Before you become too worried about this, remember that you are in a Higher class because your teacher thinks you are capable of completing the course.

Coursework and Exam

Coursework preparation

Selecting a coursework task

The SQA has produced a few coursework tasks that must be used by every school presenting students for Higher Computing Science in the first two years (2015 and 2016 exams). In later years the SQA will add to the bank of available coursework tasks.

Each task will have an emphasis on different parts of the course. One may require a website to be coded, while another may require a relational database to be designed and implemented. Every task will require you to write a computer program.

It is likely that your school will select one of the SQA tasks for you to complete. The choice should be based on the work you have covered in the most depth or on your own personal knowledge and skills.

The format of the coursework

All coursework is required to cover content from both units of the course. As a result each task will be written as two sub-tasks presented around a single scenario. Each of the sub-tasks will describe a series of stages that you should follow carefully.

The 60 marks available for the coursework are allocated to these stages as follows:
- 10 marks for analysing the information system and program requirements.
- 10 marks for designing an information system and user interface.
- 10 marks for developing and testing the designed information system.
- 10 marks for designing a modular program.
- 10 marks for developing and testing the designed modular program.
- 10 marks for reporting on the solutions you designed and implemented.

At the end of the coursework task you are required to submit a complete report that must include evidence of everything you analysed, designed, implemented, tested and reported on. Evidence could be a printout, screenshot or file. As part of your report, you will be expected to submit a diary noting the parts of the coursework you completed in each period you worked on the task.

The coursework tasks are 'open book'. Make as much use of this as you can by referring constantly to your course notes, examples of other work you have completed and the world wide web.

Preparing for the coursework

Your teacher can't disclose details of the task before you start it, but they may tell you which areas of the course you should practise in advance. Coding a website, creating a relational database and practising programming before the task will ensure that these skills are fresh.

Read through the areas of your notes referring to analysis, design, implementation and testing for both the SDD and ISDD units.

How to be successful

Each of the 10-mark sections of the coursework is graded according to the completeness and quality of your work. Read the task over and over, making sure that you have completed each stage before you move on. If you miss anything out you will automatically lose marks.

Make sure you are organised. Keep any printouts safe and organise your files carefully.

Your teacher can't show you how to carry out any part of the coursework task, but they are allowed to clarify things for you and point you in the right direction. If you don't understand an instruction, ask for it to be explained.

Try your best! Remember, the higher your coursework mark, the fewer marks you need to get in the exam to achieve your target grade.

CSS properties and values

Text

Property	Example values	Explanation
font-family	arial helvetica	Sets the selector's font.
	"times new roman"	Note that if the name of the font is longer than one word it should be enclosed in inverted commas.
font-size	medium	Sets text to small, medium, large size.
	1em	Sets text size relative to the browser's default setting.
	14px 18pt	Sets to a fixed size in pixels (px) or points (pt).
	75%	The percentage value indicates the size of text relative to a parent element.
font-weight	bold	Adjusts the thickness of each character using either text values (bold, etc.) or more accurately using numerical values (e.g. 500).
	normal	For numerical values, 400 = normal and 700 = bold.
	bolder	
	lighter	
	400	
font-style	normal	Sets styles of text (as seen in word processing applications).
	underline	
	italics	
text-decoration	underline	Works in a similar way to font-style and is commonly used to style hyperlinks.
	overline	
	line-through	
text-transform	capitalise	Changes the first letter of every word into uppercase.
	uppercase	Turns all the text to uppercase.
	lowercase	Turns all the text to lowercase.
letter-spacing	0.5em	Sets the size of the gap between each letter.
word-spacing	2em	Sets the size of the gap between each word.
word-wrap	normal	Sets text to wrap words at the end of a line.
	break-word	Sets text to split words if they are too long.
text-align	left	Text justification as found in word processing applications. Note the spelling of 'center' uses American English.
	right	
	center	
	justify	
text-indent	20px	Indents the first word of a paragraph by a distance given in px.
line-height	2	Specifies the distance between the lines in relation to the font size. So a value of 2 would be double spacing.

Colours

Property	Example values	Explanation
color background-color	blue rgb(255,67,0) #ff349f	Colours (note the American spelling in HTML and CSS) can be set on the majority of selectors using: ● a word – red, navy, yellow, black ● an rgb value – expressed as numbers between 0 and 255 (e.g. 237,129,255) or as a percentage (e.g. 60%,34%,0%). ● a hexadecimal rgb code – using either one digit (0-f) for each colour (f6b), or two digits (ff6c00).

Margins, padding and borders

Property	Example values	Explanation
margin	20 px	Sets a space in pixels around the outside of the entire selector.
margin-left margin-right margin-top margin-bottom	30 px	As above but allows for more control over which side of the selector will have the margin.
padding	40 px	Defines a blank area of space inside the boundaries of a selector.
padding-left padding-right padding-top padding-bottom	16 px	As above but allows for more control over which side of the selector will have the padded area.
border-width	3 px	Sets a border width in px around the entire selector.
border-left-width border-right-width border-top-width border-bottom-width	10 px	As above but allows for more control over the border thickness applied to each side of the selector.
border-color	red	Sets the colour of the border (note the American spelling of color).
border-style	solid dotted dashed double	Sets the appearance of the border as described by the values shown.

Positioning, floating and clear

Property	Example values	Explanation
position	static	Ensures that the selector appears in the order given in the HTML.
	relative	Takes the selector's normal (static) position and moves it relative to this point.
	absolute	Sets the selector to ignore its order in the HTML code and move to a set point on the web page.
	fixed	Similar to absolute but the selector stays in its position on the web page, even when the page is scrolled in the browser.
top bottom left right	0 px 20 px	Used in conjunction with the position property to place a selector at an exact position in the web page. Left:20px would move the selector 20 pixels in from the left.
float	left right	Moves a selector to the left or right of the page with surrounding content flowing round it.
clear	left right both	Cancels the effect of floating left or right selectors.

HTML tag reference

Document

Tag	Explanation of use
`<html>` `</html>`	The HTML tags appear at the top and bottom of every web page. They tell the browser that this is an HTML document.
`<head>` `</head>`	The head tag acts as a container for head elements. The head tag must include a `<title>` and may include `<style>`, `<base>`, `<link>`, `<meta>` and `<script>` tags.
`<title>` `</title>`	The title tag is used to enclose a title of your choice that will appear at the top of the browser when the page is viewed.
`<body>` `</body>`	The body tag encloses all the content of the web page that will be displayed by the browser.

Example	`<html>`
	　　　`<head>`
	　　　　　`<title>My Hockey Home Page</title>`
	　　　`</head>`
	　　　`<body>`
	　　　　　`<p>I have been playing hockey since the age of 6.</p>`
	　　　`</body>`
	`</html>`

Layout

Tag	Explanation of use
`<header>` `</header>`	An area at the top of a page commonly used to display the site's name and logo.
`<footer>` `</footer>`	An area at the bottom of a page often containing legal or contact details.
`<nav>` `</nav>`	Used to create an area for a website's navigation links.
`<section>` `</section>`	Defines a section or distinct area of a web page.
`<article>` `</article>`	Used to enclose an article within a web page.
`<div>` `</div>`	The division tag can be used several times throughout a document to split the HTML code into sections. Division tags are often used with CSS files to lay out a web page.
`<p>` `</p>`	The paragraph tag is used to define and enclose paragraphs of text.
` `	The break tag tells the browser to move the next object on to the next line.

Links

Tag	Explanation of use
<a> </a>	The a tag encloses an object to turn it into a hyperlink. It is used like this: <a href="http://www.rslearning.co.uk">Visit RS Learning Ltd</a>
<link>	The link tag is used to load in external sources like style sheets. It has no end tag. It is used like this: <link rel="stylesheet" href="Home Page Styles.css">

Graphics

Tag	Explanation of use
<img>	The image tag includes a link to a graphic file and tells the browser how to display the file. It is used like this: <img src="smiley.gif" alt="Smiley face" height="42" width="42">

Tables

Tag	Explanation of use
<table> </table>	The table tag is used to enclose the contents of a table.
<tr> </tr>	The table row tags enclose the data for each row of the table. If the table has three columns, each table row tag will enclose three sets of data tags: <td> </td>.
<td> </td>	The table data tags each represent a cell in the table row. All the information in a table, displayed by the browser, is enclosed by <td> </td> tags.
<thead> </thead>	The table head tag usually encloses the top row of the table. It can be used to style the headings or top row of the table differently from the rest of the table.
<tbody> </tbody>	The table body tag encloses all the rows that make up the body of the table. It can be used to style the body content of the table differently from the headings.
<colgroup> </colgroup>	The column group tag allows groups of columns to be declared and then styled. Additional <col> tags contain the information about how the columns are grouped.
Example	``` <table> <colgroup> <col style="background-color:red"> <col span="2" style="background-color:yellow"> </colgroup> <thead style="background-color:red"> <tr> <td>Name</td> <td>Wins</td> <td>Draws</td> </tr> </thead> <tbody> <tr> <td>Pars United</td> <td>29</td> <td>5</td> </tr> <tr> <td>Saints Academicals</td> <td>18</td> <td>16</td> </tr> </tbody> </table> ```

Lists

Tag	Explanation of use
<ul> </ul>	The unordered list tag creates a bullet-point list. Each bulleted item should be contained between list item tags.
<ol> </ol>	The ordered list tag creates a numbered list. Each numbered item should be contained between list item tags.
<li> </li>	The list item tags are used to enclose each item in a list.
Example	<ul> <li>Bread</li> <li>Butter</li> <li>Jam</li> </ul>

JavaScript code reference

Syntax rules

Example	Explanation

`<script>`
 	
    code goes here
 	
`</script>`
	JavaScript code is contained within the `<script>` HTML tag.

;	Each line of a script is separated using a semi-colon.
( )	Curved brackets are used to contain conditions.
{ }	Curly brackets contain one or more lines of code to be executed.
//	Comments may be added to code using a double forward slash.

JavaScript constructs

Constructs	Example code	Explanation

Assignment (integers)	`var x;`
	`x = 5;`
	
	`var count = 0;`
	
	`var num = num + count;`
		x is declared as a variable and then assigned the value 5.
		
		These two lines can be combined into one line as shown.
		
		A variable can be created and assigned values from other variables.

Assignment (strings)	`var answer = "Egypt"`
	
	`var outputString = answer + " is correct"`
		A string is assigned using " ".
		
		Strings can be concatenated using the + symbol.

Assignment (arrays)	`var books = ["paperback", "hardback", "diary", "notebook"];`
	
	`books[0] = "leaflet";`
		An array can be declared and assigned values as shown.
		
		The elements of the array are numbered (indexed), starting from 0.

Selection (if)	`if (counter>10) {bonus = pay * 1.25};`	The variable bonus is assigned a value of pay *1.25 if the counter variable is greater than 10.

Repetition (unconditional loop)	`for (num=0; num<4; num++) {`
	    `counter = counter + 1;`
	`}`
		The loop will repeat four times, counting from 0 to 3, adding on 1 each time.
		
		( ) and { } brackets are used as above.

Repetition (conditional loop)	`var num = 0;`
	
	`while (num<15) {`
	    `total = total + num; num++;`
	`}`
		This loop will repeat while the variable num is less than 15.
		
		num++ increments the variable num by 1 each time the loop is executed.

Assignment (object)	`var game = {genre: "Action", age: "15", name: "Battle Droids"};`
	
	`var gameTitle = game.name;`
		An object is created to store the properties of a computer game.
		
		A full stop is used after the object name to access a specific property.

Functions	```function addTwoNums() { var num1 = 2; var num2 = 4; var total = num1 * num2; }```	A function can be created to modularise code. Functions can be called using code or events such as a button click.
Functions (returns value)	```function addTwoNums(num1,num2) { return num1 + num2; } total = addTwoNums(5,6);```	Using parameters, a function can be used to perform a calculation and return a result. The result can then be assigned to a variable using the function as shown.
Event (button click)	`<button onclick= "addTwoNums()"> Click Me</button>`	The HTML tag <button> can be used to create a button that calls a JavaScript function when it is clicked. This is a common way of allowing the user to run your JavaScript code.
Built-in functions (random)	`num = Math.random( );`	Generates a random number between 0 and 1 and stores it in a variable.
Built-in functions (round)	`num = Math.round(5.3);`	Used to round a number to the nearest integer. In the example, num would store the value 5.
Built-in functions (max) (min)	```num1 = Math.max(1,34,87,129,3,9); num2 = Math.min(1,34,87,129,3,9);```	The max and min functions will find the largest and smallest values in a list.
Built-in functions (length)	```var text = "Computing Higher"; var textLength = text.length;```	The length function can be used to determine the number of characters in a string. textLength would equal 16 in the example.
Built-in functions (toUpperCase) (toLowerCase)	```var text = "Computing Higher"; var lower = text.toUpperCase; var upper = text.toLowerCase;```	These two functions will convert a string to lower or upper case characters.

JavaScript and HTML examples

Example code	Explanation
Using JavaScript to write content in a web page: `<p id = "textadd"> </p>` ```<script> var text = "Display this"; document.getElementById("textadd").innerHTML = text; </script>```	In the example the HTML paragraph <p> element is assigned an id. This id can be used in the code shown to write text from a variable into this element, causing it to be displayed on the web page.

Use JavaScript to handle data entered into an HTML form:	In the example the \<form\> tag is used to create two input boxes on the web page.
	When the button is clicked the function called captureForm is called.
\<body\>	The function reads the data from the form into an array called formDetails. As there were two input boxes the array created has two elements.
\<form id="myForm"\>	
First name: \<input type="text" name="firstname"\>\<br\>	
Last name: \<input type="text" name="lastname"\>\<br\>	Each array element is read into a variable. These are concatenated along with a break \<br\> tag.
\<br\>	
\</form\>	Finally, the concatenated text is written back to the web page using the \<p\> tag with the id testPara.
\<button onclick="captureForm()"\>Try it\</button\>	
\<p id="testPara"\>\</p\>	
\<script\>	
function captureForm() {	
var formDetails = document.getElementById("myForm");	
var firstName = formDetails.elements[0].value;	
var surname = formDetails.elements[1].value;	
textOut = firstName + "\<br\>" + surname;	
document.getElementById("testPara").innerHTML = textOut;	
}	
\</script\>	
\</body\>	

Course Assessment Specification

Software Design and Development

Topic	Higher
Languages and environments	Description of the key characteristics of the following language types: ● low-level ● high-level ● procedural ● declarative ● object-oriented.

Computational constructs	● Parameter passing (value and reference, formal and actual).
	
	● Scope, local and global variables.
	
	● Sub-programs/routines, defined by their name and arguments (inputs and outputs), including:
	  ● functions
	  ● procedures
	  ● methods.

Data types and structures	● String. ● Numeric (integer and real) variables. ● Boolean variables. ● 1-D arrays, records. ● Sequential files (open, create, read, write, close).
Testing and documenting solutions	● Constructing a test plan. ● Comprehensive testing. ● Syntax, execution and logic errors. ● Dry runs, trace tables, breakpoints.
Algorithm specification	Analysis, exemplification and implementation of algorithms, including: ● input validation ● linear search ● find minimum and maximum ● count occurrences. Analysis of other algorithms of a similar complexity.

Low-level operations and computer architecture	• Virtual machines.
	• Emulators.
	• Mobile devices.
	Use of binary to represent and store:
	• integers and real numbers
	• characters
	• instructions (machine code)
	• graphics (bit-mapped and vector)
	• sound
	• video.
	Computer architecture (trends and implications):
	• processor (registers, ALU, control unit), cache, memory, buses (data and address), interfaces.

Software and Information Systems Design and Development

Topic	Higher
Design notations	• Structure diagram.
	• Entity relationship (ER) diagram.
	• Data dictionary.
	• Pseudocode.
	• Wire framing.
	• Other contemporary design notations.
Development methodologies	Iterative phases of development process: analysis, design, implementation, testing, documentation, evaluation, maintenance.
	Development methodologies:
	• rapid application development
	• top-down/step-wise refinement
	• agile methodologies.
Contemporary developments	Exemplification of trends in the development of:
	• software development languages
	• software development environments
	• intelligent systems
	• online systems.
User interface	• Usability.
	• Accessibility.

Information Systems Design and Development

Topic	Higher
Structures and links (databases)	• Database structures: relational. • Primary keys, including compound keys. • Relationships (one-to-one, one-to-many, many-to-many). • Complex database operations (including queries, forms, reports, calculating).
Structures and links (web-based)	• Site structure: multi-level. • Page structure, including head, title, body. • Cascading style sheets. • Meta tags. • Dynamic web pages, database-driven websites. • Interactive web pages.

Media types	Compression:
	• lossy and lossless compression techniques, applied to:
	  • sound
	  • graphics
	  • video.

Coding	Exemplification and implementation of coding to create and modify information systems, including the use of: • scripting (database/web pages) • client-side scripting • server-side scripting • optimisation (web search (crawlers) and efficiency of coding).
Testing	• Beta testing. • Usability. • Compatibility issues (including memory and storage requirements, OS compatibility).

Purpose, functionality, users	• Descriptions of purpose.
	• Interactions of information systems with:
	  • human users: expert, novice, age-range
	  • other software: search engines.

Technical implementation (hardware requirements)	• Input and output devices. • Processor type, number and speed (Hz). • Memory (RAM, ROM, cache). • Device type (including desktop, laptop, tablet, smartphone).
Technical implementation (software requirements)	• Operating systems. • Licensing. • Proprietary vs open source. • Portability. Description and exemplification of current trends in operating systems design.

Technical implementation (storage)	• Distributed and offline storage.
	• Backup systems and strategies.
	• Capacity (in appropriate units).
	• Rewritable, read-only.
	• Interface type.
	• Data transfer speed.
	Storage devices:
	• built-in, external
	• magnetic, optical
	• solid state.
	Description and exemplification of current trends in storage systems.
Technical implementation (networking/ connectivity)	Cloud systems and server provision:
	• public, private, hybrid
	• cloud-based services
	• web hosting.
	Description and exemplification of current trends in networking and connectivity.
Security risks	• Spyware, phishing, keylogging.
	• Online fraud, identity theft.
	• DOS (Denial of Service) attacks.
Security precautions	• Encryption.
	• Digital certificates and signatures.
	• Server-side validation of online form data.
	• Biometrics.
Legal implications	Detailed descriptions and implications of:
	• Computer Misuse Act
	• Copyright, Designs and Patents Act (plagiarism)
	• Communications Act
	• Regulation of Investigatory Powers Act.
Environmental implications	• Lifetime carbon footprint (manufacture, use, disposal).
	• Benefits.
Economic and social impact	• Economic: competitive advantage, global marketplace, business costs, maintainability, scalability.
	• Social: censorship and freedom of speech, privacy and encryption, global citizenship, online communities.

Answers to Questions

Chapter 1

1 High level language programs can be compiled to run on different computer processors with different instruction sets. (1 mark) Binary (low level language) programs will run on only one computer with a single instruction set. (1 mark)
2 Object-oriented. (1 mark) A touchscreen application will consist of objects that are selected or dragged by means of touch. (1 mark)
3 Without a strict set of rules it would be impossible to create a compiler to convert the high level language to binary as the user could enter instructions any way they like. (1 mark)
4 All data and instructions in a computer system must be stored and processed as binary as the computer's hardware is built to store and process only binary. (1 mark)

Chapter 2

Answers are given in Python.

```
1  # Ask the user to enter the number of pairs of shoes they have
   numOfShoes = 0
   numOfShoes = int(input("How many pairs of shoes will you sell?"))
   # Use input validation to ensure the number entered is more than 0
   while numOfShoes <= 0:
       print("Please enter a value greater than 0")
       numOfShoes = int(input("Re-enter the number of pairs of shoes"))

   # Set up an array, with the correct number of elements,
   # to store the cost of each pair of shoes
   shoeCost = [0.0] * numOfShoes

   # Use a loop to enter the cost of each pair of shoes
   for loop in range(numOfShoes):
       shoeCost[loop] = float(input("Enter the cost (in pounds) of the next pair of shoes"))
       # Use input validation to ensure the cost entered is more than 0
       while  shoeCost[loop] <= 0:
           print("Please enter a value greater than 0")
           shoeCost[loop] = float(input("Re-enter the cost"))

   # Calculate and display the total cost
   totalCost = 0.0
   for loop in range(numOfShoes):
       totalCost = totalCost + shoeCost[loop]
   print("The total cost of the shoes is",totalCost)
```

2

```
# Set up two real arrays each 7 elements in size
parent = [-1]*7
child = [-1]*7

# Unconditional loop * 7, once for each day of the week
for loop in range(7):
    # Input validation to ensure hours entered are between 0 and 24
    while parent[loop] < 0 or parent[loop] > 24:
        parent[loop] = float(input("Please enter a value for the parent"))
        if parent[loop] < 0 or parent[loop] > 24:
            print("Please enter a value between 0 and 24")
    while child[loop] < 0 or child[loop] > 24:
        child[loop] = float(input("Please enter a value for the child"))
        if child[loop] < 0 or child[loop] > 24:
            print("Please enter a value between 0 and 24")

# Set up the initial total for each person
parentTotal = 0
childTotal = 0

# Use a loop to calculate a running total for each person
for loop in range(7):
    parentTotal = parentTotal + parent[loop]
    childTotal = childTotal + child[loop]

# Display who watches the most TV
print("Parent watches ",parentTotal," hours of TV.")
print("Child watches ",childTotal," hours of TV.")
if parentTotal > childTotal:
    print("The parent watches more TV.")
elif parentTotal < childTotal:
    print("The child watches the most TV.")
else:
    print("Both watch the same amount of TV.")
```

3

```
# Create an array of 1 element.  We will add more as required.
soilSamples = [0.0]*1

# Create a Boolean variable to control the conditional loop
anotherSample = True
# Create a variable to keep count of the number of entries
count = 0
# Create a variable to store the average pH
averagePH = 0

# Loop while anotherSample = True
while anotherSample:
    # Enter the pH sample
    print("Please enter the pH of sample ",count+1)
    soilSamples[count] = float(input("Now enter the PH for this sample"))
    # Use input validation to ensure the value is between 0 and 14
    while soilSamples[count] < 0 or soilSamples[count] > 14:
        print("Invalid pH value!")
        soilSamples[count] = float(input("Enter the PH for this sample again"))

    # Ask the user if they wish to enter another value
    print("Do you wish to enter another sample")
    anotherSample = input("Enter True or press return")

    # If yes add one to the counter and one element to the array
    if anotherSample:
        count = count + 1
        soilSamples.append(0.0)
```

```
# Now add up the values and divide to find the average
for loop in range(count+1):
    averagePH = averagePH + soilSamples[loop]
averagePH = averagePH /(count+1)

# Display the result
if averagePH < 7:
    print("The soil has an average acidic pH")
elif averagePH > 7:
    print("The soil has an average alkaline pH")
else:
    print("The soil has a neutral average pH")
```

Answers

Chapter 3

1 The program requires three arrays and one variable:
   - Light meter readings – array of real numbers. (1 mark)
   - Reading dates – an array of strings. (1 mark)
   - Average meter reading – real number variable. (1 mark)
   - List of dates when within 0.3 of average – array of strings. (1 mark)
2 Global. (1 mark) Small programs are unlikely to have subroutines. (1 mark)
3 If a variable name is mistakenly used twice the value initially stored in the variable will be overwritten when it is used elsewhere in the program. (1 mark)
4 The wages are used but not altered (1 mark) and should therefore be passed by value (1 mark).
5 If an array were passed by value a copy would be created. (1 mark) This could cause issues with available resources (memory) causing the program to crash. (1 mark)

Answers

Chapter 4

1 a) Count occurrences (1 mark) – the program counts the 'number of tracks' that are less than 120 seconds long.
   b) Find maximum (1 mark) and find minimum (1 mark) – the app 'displays the fastest and slowest speeds' recorded.
   c) Input validation (1 mark) – the app records only values over 10. Linear search (1 mark) – the app displays 'all the speeds' that are over 30mph.
2 The values stored are 1, 56, 83 and 90. (1 mark)
   The values stored in the array are 1,56,3,54,26,83,1,5,90,2,5. The algorithm begins by storing the first value stored in the array. The first value is replaced by the next largest value: 56. 56 is not replaced until the next largest number is found: 83. 90 then replaces 83.
3 Two input statements should be added to the beginning of the algorithm to allow the user to enter two values. (1 mark) The IF statement can then be rewritten to include these values. (1 mark)

```
IF weights[counter] >= lower AND weights[counter] <= upper THEN
```

Answers

Chapter 5

1 The test plan should have included tests to check that the app carried out tasks in an acceptable period of time. (1 mark)

2 To test a program fully involves testing every possible input. With many programs there may be an almost infinite number of possible inputs, making it impossible to test them all. (1 mark)

3 An execution error. (1 mark)

4 The test data should describe the following:
   - Normal data – an integer between 1 and 12, for example 7. (1 mark)
   - Extreme data – 1 and 12. (1 mark)
   - Exceptional data – a real number, text or a value outwith 1 and 12, for example 3.5, x, -5. (1 mark)

5 Static testing is performed without running/executing the program. The results of static testing are predicted. (1 mark) Dynamic testing is performed by executing the program with set test data. The results of the testing are actual recorded events. (1 mark)

Answers

Chapter 6

1 The answer below is given in pseudocode.

```
OPEN FILE "raceTimes"                  (1 mark for opening file)
FOR counter FROM 1 to 5                (1 mark for unconditional
                                        loop)
   RECEIVE time FROM (REAL) KEYBOARD   (1 mark for user input)
   SEND time TO raceTimes              (1 mark for writing to file)
END FOR
CLOSE FILE "raceTimes"                 (1 mark for closing file)
```

2 Name of file: name. (1 mark)
   File type: plain text file, 'txt'. (1 mark)
   Connection type: read only, 'r'. (1 mark)

3 The answer for this question will vary depending on the programming language used. Award yourself 1 mark for completing the task. You can use the internet to search for a similar example to check your syntax.

Answers

Chapter 7

1 Any suitable example of returning to an earlier stage of the process. For example, after testing the process will return to the implementation stage to fix errors. (1 mark)

2 Documentation is used by programmers to decipher the purpose of each section of code. Without proper documentation the process of finding and coding the required fix/upgrade will take longer. (1 mark)

3 Adaptive. (1 mark)

4 Wire frames are used to design layouts by noting the position of objects. They therefore cannot be used to design the logical solution to a problem. (1 mark)

5 The client's software is produced – and therefore delivered – faster. (1 mark) The client has increased input during the project. (1 mark)

⇨

⇨

6 The inflexibility of the waterfall method, the seven stages carried out in order, is unsuitable for developments that often rely on ideas and imagination during the development. (1 mark)

7 Any suitable example of an app being 'improved'. For example, in a game improvements would include the introduction of new levels, new objects added, etc. (1 mark)

Answers

Chapter 8

1 A computer uses transistors to process data. Transistors have two states, on and off (1 and 0). (1 mark)

2 Storing all numbers, including integers, as floating point values is inefficient as floating point notation usually requires more storage than integers. (1 mark)

3 101001000 (1 mark)

256	128	64	32	16	8	4	2	U
1	0	1	0	0	1	0	0	0

4 The smallest negative number is achieved when the left-hand negative column is 1 and the remaining columns are all 0.

−128	64	32	16	8	4	2	U
1	0	0	0	0	0	0	0

The largest positive number is achieved when the left-hand column is 0 and the remaining columns are all 1.

−128	64	32	16	8	4	2	U
0	1	1	1	1	1	1	1

The range therefore is −128 to 127. (2 marks: 1 mark for each value)

5 As −212 is outside the range calculated in Question 4, a ninth column is required.

−256	128	64	32	16	8	4	2	U
1	0	0	1	0	1	1	0	0

6 = −512 + 64 + 16 + 2 = −430

−512	256	128	64	32	16	8	4	2	U
1	0	0	1	0	1	0	0	1	0

7 As an 8-bit code, ASCII can store only 256 different characters, whereas the 16-bit Unicode can store 65 536 different characters.

8 Size of file = resolution × colour depth
Size of file = 3000 × 2400 × 24 bit (1 mark)
Size of file = 172,800,000 bits
Size of file = 21,600,000 bytes
Size of file = 21,093.75 KB
Size of file = 20.60 MB (1 mark for conversion to appropriate units)
Note that it is advisable to round off your answer to two or more decimal places, as one decimal place would create too large an error.

9 24-bit colour is being used. (1 mark) The code shows rgb (red, green, blue) values being used between 0 and 255, signifying that 8 bits is being used to store each colour's value. 8 bits × 3 colours = 24 bits.

10 16 bits = 65 536 possible values when sampling the amplitude of the wave. (1 mark)

11 Size of file = resolution × colour depth × frame rate × time (secs)
Size of file = 1920 × 1080 × 16 bit × 20 fps × 180 seconds (1 mark)
Size of file = 13.90 GB (1 mark for conversion to appropriate units)

Answers

Chapter 9

1. The read line is activated in the memory read steps, while the write line is activated in the memory write steps. (1 mark)
   In a memory write operation the data being written is set up on the MDR before being transferred. (1 mark)

2. ALU – will be involved when the two values are compared as this is a logical operation. (1 mark)
   Control unit – will control the reading of the two values and the instruction, and will then instruct the ALU to carry out the comparison. (1 mark)
   Registers – the values being compared will be stored within the processor (1 mark)

3. One mark for any one of the following:
   - The interface will convert the analogue sound to digital.
   - The interface will convert the serial data to parallel.
   - The interface will compensate for the difference in the voltage of the microphone and the computer.

4. Maximum memory = $2^{24} \times 32$ bits (1 mark for initial line of calculation)
   Maximum memory = 536,870,912 bits
   Maximum memory = 64 MB (1 mark for conversion to correct units)

5. One mark for any one of the following:
   - Increased data bus widths result in more data being transferred in one read or write operation.
   - Multiple core processors allow for more than one instruction to be processed simultaneously.
   - Increased cache memory improves performance by preloading instructions and then transferring them faster to the processor than is possible from the main memory.

6. Mairi could use a virtual machine to simulate an Apple environment on her Windows PC. (1 mark)

Answers

Chapter 10

1. Different IDEs may offer different features, or one feature may be better in one IDE than in another. (1 mark)

2. The user will be familiar with the development environment, which may save time as the user will not have to become familiar with a new environment. (1 mark)

3. A breakpoint allows the programmer temporarily to stop the program from executing. (1 mark)
   This allows the programmer to examine the values of variables at this point and compare them against expected results. (1 mark)

4. Processing the image of the number plate requires a computer system. (1 mark) The system is intelligent because it then accesses a central database to search for the car's insurance details. (1 mark)

5. Bookings and availability for the rooms will be stored in the hotel's database. The booking website must therefore be linked to the database in order to inform the user whether or not the booking they have requested is possible. (1 mark)

6. One mark each for any two of the following:
   - Automating their booking system reduces the number of staff required to process bookings.
   - An online booking system provides instant feedback to the user and will therefore increase bookings.
   - An online booking system is available at all times of the day and night, increasing the number of bookings.
   - An online system has a larger potential number of clients, which increases the number of bookings.

Answers

Chapter 12

1 One sports team will consist of more than one student, and one student may play in more than one sports team. (1 mark)

2 If the same field(s) are present in more than one table, errors are created when only one copy of the data is updated. (1 mark)

3 One mark for each of the following:
- All five entities included in the diagram.
- All correct relationships included.
- Cardinality all correct.

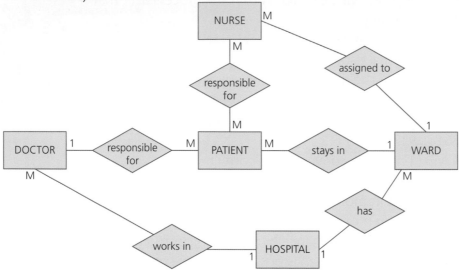

4 One mark for each of the following:
- All four entities included in the diagram.
- All correct relationships included.
- Cardinality all correct.
- The unique ID of each comic is shown to be created from the name and issue attributes.
- The characters have a superpower attribute.

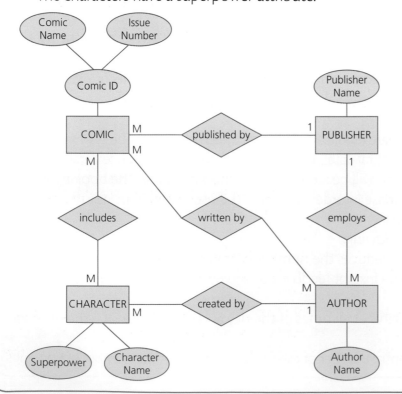

5 One mark for each line below:

```
SELECT Forename, Surname
     FROM Reporters
     ORDER BY Surname ASC;
```

6 One mark for each line below:

```
INSERT INTO Reporters
     VALUES ('0348','David','Presley','Sports','003');
```

7 One mark for each line below:

```
UPDATE Newspapers
     SET ProducedIn = 'Paisley'
     WHERE PaperID = 002;
```

8 A one-to-many relationship. (1 mark)
9 Create a query with the following fields:
   • Newspapers.paperName and criteria = "The Daily Read" (1 mark)
   Select three fields from Reporters table: (1 mark)
   • Reporters.FirstName
   • Reporters.Surname
   • Reporters.Genre
   And then create a report using the results of the query. (1 mark)

Answers

Chapter 13

1 For the author meta tag: (1 mark)

```
<meta name = "author" content="Gillian">
```

For the description (note that the context text may vary slightly in your answer): (1 mark)

```
<meta name = "description" content="My website about my pet
Labradoodle">
```

For keywords (at least four of the list below is required to gain a mark): (1 mark)

```
<meta name = "keywords" content="dog, labradoodle, feeding, walks,
brush, cut, coat">
```

2 High definition wire frame. (1 mark)
3 <body> (1 mark)
4 The text will be displayed using the <p> tag style. (1 mark) Although ID styles have a higher priority than tag styles, the ID is applied to the <div> tag and not to the <p> tag. Therefore, the <p> tag will use the tag style defined in the style sheet. (1 mark)
5 A button would be implemented using a programming language like JavaScript, (1 mark) whereas the changing layout would require the use of HTML and multiple cascading style sheets (1 mark).
6 The items of clothing are stored in a database. (1 mark)
   The page is interactive because clicking on an item of clothing changes the content of the page. (1 mark)
   The repeating clothing graphics in the area are an example of dynamic content. (1 mark)
7 The program code (or script) used to generate the page resides on the web server and not on the user's computer. (1 mark)

Answers

Chapter 14

1 Any three from: (1 mark)
   - The names should be grouped together.
   - The input boxes should be increased in size.
   - Radio buttons should be used for Sex instead of an input box.
   - Radio buttons or drop down menus should be used for age ranges.
2 Add subtitles to the video. (1 mark)

Answers

Chapter 15

1 Without compression the video files would be too large to download to the user's browser within an appropriate period of time.
2 Run length and LZW encoding work well where the same colours or patterns of colour repeat. (1 mark) In a 24-bit photograph there may be over 17 million different colours of pixels, meaning the likelihood of colour or pattern repetition is very small (1 mark).
3 Run length encoding (1 mark) is the most suitable as the file contains long runs of consecutive pixels that are all the same colour (1 mark).
4 Lossless. (1 mark) The technique described stores complete information about each repeating pattern of characters in the text file. The original file could be rebuilt using this information. (1 mark)
5 Lots of fast movement means that each frame will be markedly different from the previous frame. (1 mark) This means that almost all of the frame following each I-frame must be stored in full, meaning only minimal compression is achieved. (1 mark)

Answers

Chapter 16

1 a) This is client-side scripting (1 mark) as the code is embedded in the HTML being viewed at the client's end (1 mark).
   b) Users can view the source code of the web page (1 mark), meaning that they can look at the answers to the quiz (1 mark).
2 Firewall. (1 mark)
3 If the styles are stored externally it reduces the file size of the HTML document, increasing its download speed. (1 mark) If the link is near the top then the styles may be used immediately, meaning the page content can begin loading. (1 mark)
4 The page will load more slowly than it should. (1 mark) The page could be optimised by deleting the unused styles from the code. (1 mark)
5 Some of the games may require a newer version of the Flash plugin. (1 mark) The solution is to update the Flash plugin on David's computer. (1 mark)

Answers

Chapter 17

1 A hacker who gains access to the stored files could easily delete data from all of the hard disk drives in the array. This would delete the backup copies as well as the original. (1 mark)

2 Eventually the older phones will not have the hardware requirements necessary to run the latest software. (1 mark)

3 Any one from:
   • increased number of potential users
   • increased accessibility (possible use on portable devices)
   • economic benefits from greater number of users
   • reduced development costs as multiple versions of software nor required
   • reduced maintenance as one version of the software
     (any one 1 mark)

4 Cloud storage could be accessed by the phone allowing access to significantly more data. (1 mark)

5 Private storage (1 mark) would be used as neither the files shared between the offices nor the files accessible to the client would be publicly available (1 mark).

Answers

Chapter 18

1 Spyware. (1 mark)

2 Denial of service attack. (1 mark)

3 The keys are paired as one key provides the means to unencrypt data encrypted by the other key. (1 mark)

4 Ensure that the key is contained within a verified public certificate. (1 mark)

5 Biometric data is very difficult to forge (1 mark) in comparison to a PIN or password, which could be guessed (1 mark).

Answers

Chapter 19

1 Copyright, Design and Patents Act. (1 mark) Samalia is reproducing the newspaper's articles without its permission. (1 mark)

2 Computer Misuse Act. (1 mark) Derek has hacked into his account and altered information. (1 mark)

3 Communications Act. (1 mark) Ross is in possession of equipment capable of illegally obtaining communications services. (1 mark)

4 Communications Act (1 mark): Carolann is using another user's Wi-Fi signal without permission (1 mark).
   Copyright Designs and Patents Act (1 mark): Carolann is illegally copying films (1 mark).
   Regulation of Investigatory Powers Act (1 mark): the scale of Carolann's 'substantial' operation may mean that her activities are monitored using RIPA (1 mark).

Answers

Chapter 20

1 Scalability. (1 mark)

2 The phone manufacture requires energy and materials (could also mention shipping). (1 mark)
  The phone must be charged regularly, which requires energy. (1 mark)
  When the phone is replaced it should be recycled, which uses energy. (1 mark)

3 Economic: a review (either good or bad) will influence the success of the business. (1 mark)
  Social: the hotel must allow free speech but must ensure that the review option is not abused (e.g. by the leaving of offensive comments). (1 mark)

4 Any three from the following (1 mark each):
  - The potential customer base is increased.
  - Sales can be made at any time.
  - Customers can see reviews of items, which may encourage purchases.
  - Customers can compare items and more easily find the one they want.
  - Customers can choose search criteria to easily find the items they want.